P. 88 - JUNIPERUS
        UIRGINIANA
P. 152-

PAINTING THE ROSES WHITE

~ Confessions of ~
an Amateur Gardener

BARBARA WENZEL

Angus&Robertson
An imprint of HarperCollins*Publishers*

AN ANGUS & ROBERTSON BOOK
An imprint of HarperCollinsPublishers

First published in Australia in 1989 by McCulloch Publishing Pty Ltd
This revised edition published in 1993 by
CollinsAngus&Robertson Publishers Pty Limited (ACN 009 913 517)
A division of HarperCollinsPublishers (Australia) Pty Limited
25 Ryde Road, Pymble NSW 2073, Australia

HarperCollinsPublishers (New Zealand) Limited
31 View Road, Glenfield, Auckland 10, New Zealand

HarperCollinsPublishers Limited
77-85 Fulham Palace Road, London W6 8JB, United Kingdom

National Library of Australia
Cataloguing-in-Publication data:

Wenzel, Barbara, 1941– .
    Painting the roses white.

    New ed.

    Bibliography.

    ISBN 0 207 18005 9.

    1. Gardening – Humour. 2. Gardening – Anecdotes.
    I. Title.

635

The publishers have attempted to contact all copyright
holders of material quoted within this book, and welcome approaches
from any copyright holder they have been unable to contact.

Cover photograph by Gerry Whitmont
Printed in Australia by Griffin Paperbacks

5 4 3 2 1
97 96 95 94 93

Contents

In The
Beginning

*M*y gardening career did not begin until after I was married. While not uncommon, this late start put me at a disadvantage, if the literature of gardening is any guide. Most of the books written by real gardeners open with a description which varies somewhat in detail but includes as a matter of course an account of hereditary estates of great beauty and sensitive instruction from a horticulturally gifted parent. I can't help feeling that this constitutes a run-up start. The obvious disadvantage of a later education is that, for most amateurs like myself, it means gardens are put together during the phase of blind ignorance, frequently with disastrous and expensive results. As Christopher Lloyd has observed, most people are pitchforked into gardening when they notice that the honeymoon cottage has some land around the edges. Clearly the thing to do is to plant something in it . By the time one has read enough to learn that the graceful little sapling bought for the front garden has a mature height of 36 metres, it may be difficult to make out the words on the page as light struggles to reach past its trunk. I do not intend these remarks as a criticism of my upbringing. We did receive more than our share of instruction in many fields: it is just that horticulture was not among them. Until I had my own quarter-acre (probably closer to eighth-acre at first), plants impinged upon my consciousness not at all. Details of my parents' garden escaped me entirely, except for some tomato plants, remarkable only because of the eye-catching home-made cloches which covered them, serving a purpose which remained obscure to me. Another much earlier and dim image is of my grandmother's house, where a myriad of potted plants of exceptional ugliness (I suspect variegated begonias) squatted malignantly on every available surface. I have wondered since if they were artificial—I never saw one in flower. My grandmother did water them, but this is inconclusive; a vein of eccentricity surfaces from time to time in the family folklore.

With a mind quite uncluttered then by any knowledge of the habits and requirements of plants, let alone the notion of garden design, I embarked upon my first garden with all the skill and enthusiasm of an absolute beginner.

Our first house was a small, rather badly renovated Victorian terrace which we thought was beautiful. It boasted a striped semi-circular awning over the front door which seemed to me to be the last word in sophistication. There was a tiny front garden and a marginally bigger one at the back which was half covered in stained, cracked concrete and featured a rotary clothes hoist centre stage.

Dimly aware that this was not an ideal configuration for a garden, our first structural change was to remove the clothesline and install a small shed of the metallic variety, so designed that it was physically impossible to open the sliding door without rending apart the entire edifice. The blinding silver sheen of this improvement still didn't seem quite right so we painted it—and the concrete slab which connected it to the house—a very white white. The effect was not unlike the polar bear enclosure at the zoo, but we arranged a tableau of potted azaleas (all pink) and retired to admire the result.

I should explain at this point that although I employ the plural pronoun quite frequently, my husband's contribution to all gardening activities is largely confined to the final stage—admiring the result. He has been known to do occasional heavy work, shifting pots and even wielding a mattock, especially in the early days. On one memorable occasion, justifying another escape to the golf-course, he did announce that he had done some selective weeding (a phrase which has entered the family lexicon) but it was a never-to-be-repeated experiment. He appears to have assumed more of the role of a Harold Nicholson in the garden—that of grand strategist.

Our next and somewhat more successful move was to cover the concrete with old brick pavers. This was such an improvement that when confronted ever since with some unpleasing surface in the garden I have covered it with old brick pavers with never a regret. The colours and texture, and patterns, both formal and informal, that can be devised with them are a deeply satisfying background for most plantings in most types of gardens.

Having dealt, we felt, in a masterly fashion with the bones of the garden's design we could now turn our attention to the planting. It was at this point that I began to suspect that I did not have my husband's undivided attention on the subject. After twenty years, my suspicion has become a conviction and I have long since given up trying to interest him in reading plant catalogues, visiting nurseries or other related activities. I know a lost cause when I see one. However, for me it was the beginning of a life-long addiction to all the trappings of gardening.

Horticultural shows, plant nurseries, familiar and exotic magazines and books have filled many hours and vacuumed out my wallet. I can see little prospect of change.

In my entire gardening career the biggest disappointment, and one from which I have never quite recovered, came quite early on. This involved the dawning realization that plants do not flower continuously and in perpetuity. Apart from a hazy notion of bulbs and flowering trees being in some way seasonal in their display, my impression of all plants was that one put them firmly in place and away they went. Easy. Water them, yes, but that was the extent of human intervention. Forever, more or less. Half-witted though that may sound, I believe that it wouldn't be too difficult to find some benighted souls who still harbour this halcyon view of the ways of plants. Never disabuse them of this notion; life seems much bleaker without it.

Only momentarily deterred by the bad news of seasons and limited lifespan (. . . Annuals? Pull them out and throw them away? Really?), I began my first garden.

I started with a piece of pure vandalism. A large, old, beautiful pale pink camellia which had doubtless been doing yeoman's service since Federation was hauled out and discarded. Not dramatic (read 'showy') enough. In its place went a large *Camellia japonica* 'The Czar'. The contrast of its red flowers against the white wall and black shutters pleased me enormously.

In a dead straight line in front of it went a row of pink azaleas. I remember being particularly fond of a salmon pink and white one called 'Madame Auguste Haarens'. There were quite a lot of these, and they were as ill-matched a companion for 'The Czar' as the good mevrouw herself would have been. The colours must have shrieked at each other; I was oblivious. I liked both plants individually; at that point there was no other consideration.

I then spent some time laboriously digging up little weeds which sprang up with dogged persistence in front of my row of azaleas, and replacing them with punnets of white primulas. In rows, naturally. One or two of the weeds which I'd missed grew to maturity and flowered. They were white primulas. I wouldn't mind admitting to this elementary error if I thought it was the last time I'd made it but I'm sure I still do it regularly.

On the other side of the minute patch of lawn reared a large Lillypilly (*Acmena smithii*). These trees are so common in suburban Melbourne that I think the planting of them must at some stage have been compulsory. I am never quite sure how I feel about them; certainly they are very dirty trees in that they always seem to be shedding some part of their anatomy (berries, twigs or fluff) with the greatest prodigality. I have never had a garden which didn't include at least one of the genus, invariably of the purple-berried variety. These berries become a positive menace when transported far and wide as a squashed purple ooze on the sole of a shoe. Another unattractive and inevitable feature is the lumpish diseased appearance of many of the leaves; this I am told is caused by the presence of an insect, appropriately named the 'pimple psyllid', the control or elimination of which is apparently well-nigh impossible. Scale also appear to find this tree irresistible. That said, the old Lillypilly is a reliable evergreen, usually of pleasing mature shape and infinitely tolerant of drought, neglect and the tortures of topiary. One thing that must be accepted, though, is that the ground underneath a Lillypilly belongs to the tree, and will remain arid and inhospitable to other plants despite herculean efforts at watering and fertilizing. This is just what I didn't accept at first, and I planted two *Camellia japonica* 'Elegans' (lipstick pink this time) in shallow holes that I scratched out of the dry root mass at the foot of the tree. I was disappointed when they failed to thrive. It was a miracle they survived at all. Two cumquats in pots were bought for either side of the front door. That was twenty years ago. They have moved with us and still flank our front door. Some years ago I thought they were starting to look a little seedy, so we bought some larger tubs and tackled the job of re-potting. We used trowels, long thin shovels, a carving knife, jets of water, ropes—in fact everything but a stick of dynamite. They didn't budge—I swear that the roots have grown into the cement. In the end we simply hosed out as much of the old soil as we could, refilled the tiny spaces not occupied by roots with fresh soil, compost and Osmocote and left them in peace. They appear quite content, if a little geriatric. But in their youth and guarding the front door under the striped awning they were quite beautiful. I still think that potted citrus have a marvellously lush and fertile look and bring a whiff of Versailles and the Alhambra, even if they have become something of a cliché. Today, I think I would use oranges rather than cumquats, although in our cool Melbourne climate, oranges seem to be much harder to coax into sufficient fertility for the required exotic effect.

Having finished the front garden, I unfortunately happened upon an article about feature trees in lawns. The photograph which really caught my eye (it must have had the most blossoms) was of a weeping cherry. Either the article was insufficiently informative or I concentrated on the pictures and skimmed over the text—a habit which I regret to say has not been entirely eradicated. Certainly, the fact that these trees were specially grafted didn't register at all. I just knew that I couldn't continue on through life without a weeping cherry featuring in our sweeping expanse of some two and a half square metres of lawn.

I bought a cherry tree and a bag of weights, the proper function of which is to carry fishing lines to the ocean floor. The cherry was duly planted and each branch of the unfortunate tree was festooned with bits of twine and sinkers. The branches did not weep gracefully like the ones in the picture; 'spreadeagled' was more the word which sprang to mind. Friends, doubtfully eyeing this apparition, did enquire tentatively about the end result. Time and growth, I confidently predicted, would see the emergence of an arched and graceful shape instead of the admittedly rather squat and curious vision before them.

The tree struggled on for years, bowed down by the ridiculous sinkers until some visitor, with more knowledge and sense than I, firmly removed them and threw them away. I fear this intervention came a little late.

The cherry tree is still there. Occasionally I drive past our old house and take a surreptitious look. The tree's habit of growth is one previously unknown in the genus *Prunus*. It contrives to simultaneously sprawl and hunch on the almost obscured lawn. Why the present owners haven't removed it, I can't imagine. Possibly they're still trying to work out what it is.

Having established my feature tree, there was little further improvement that I could wreak on the front garden. My attention turned to the back. So far, all we had was another minute patch of scruffy lawn, some attractive brick paving, a few potted azaleas and the new white shed. A narrow strip of dust and weeds which had once been a flower bed edged the lawn, backed by a bare wooden fence. The scope for improvement here was considerable. Fired with the success of the red Czar against the white wall in the front garden, I decided that a red rose was just the thing for the shed. Somehow I acquired a coloured catalogue of roses, thereby taking the first step towards an addiction to which I am still hopelessly in thrall. I simply cannot resist sending off for, poring over and, regrettably, buying from all manner of nursery catalogues. No species of flora is too obscure and no address too remote to escape my request for your mail order list please (S.A.E. enclosed).

In the Beginning

This first of a thousand catalogues was a glossy, highly coloured affair, much given to specially priced collections of assorted favourites. It appeared to be mandatory that no two roses were the same colour and that all were hybrid teas. This didn't worry me in the least as I didn't know there was any other sort. I agonized for days over the choice (now it's more likely to be weeks). What about 'Papa Meilland'? It was the right colour, sounded both French and folksy (always a winning combination), and was perfumed. It also had the biggest picture. Or 'Super Star', the colour of which could apparently be spotted three blocks away. In the end, swayed by descriptions of red-black velvet blooms in great profusion, I settled for 'Blackboy'. 'Queen Elizabeth' and 'Pascali' were added to the list to complete the red, pink and white colour scheme which was clearly becoming something of an *idée fixe*.

I sent off the order and in due course the roses arrived in the post, casually wrapped in a bit of plastic. Twenty years later, this process still makes me nervous. How can living plants be shipped off like a lot of corpses, entombed in boxes lost in the labyrinth of the postal system for indefinite periods, and still show signs of life at the other end, let alone grow and thrive? The fact that they very frequently do thrive still seems to me frankly miraculous. As a beginner the whole thing reduced me to panic, a not infrequent reaction of mine during anything remotely resembling a crisis. Tearing the clearly dead sticks from their inadequate shroud, I rushed them out to the garden and forced their roots into shallow holes I scrabbled to receive them. Soil preparation never came into it; nor did aspect. The shed at least faced west, so the 'Blackboy' should have had a chance. It did survive but was never the glorious mass of dark velvet I was hoping for and remained spindly and dispirited till we left that house five years later. As I had forced its roots into a few inches of builders' rubble and left it to get on with life, it is not surprising that it never showed much enthusiasm. The 'Pascali' went into a corner where I wanted a white rose. This was a deeply shaded spot facing south so it too, was a disappointment. The 'Queen Elizabeth', on the other hand, did splendidly, planted as it was at the very front of the small bed which happened to face north. The soil must have been good as it grew prodigiously. Unfortunately, nothing that I subsequently planted in that bed, like violas and alyssum, exceeded 15 centimetres, so the 'Queen Elizabeth' looked a little out of proportion, ranging up to almost two metres with all the grace of a tank stand. I did love the flowers, though. Properly placed at the back of a border, with plenty of cover in front to hide those awful legs, the pure and glowing pink of the roses can lift a colour scheme as few other pinks can. And it certainly is a good 'doer', a quality I am coming to value more and more highly, especially in a small suburban garden.

Buying and planting continued at an ever increasing tempo. Magpie-like, I was attracted to flowering plants of bright colour or rather obvious charm—such as giant delphiniums and petunias, daisies and lobelia. In they all went, into the tiny beds around the fence, without the slightest regard for size, soil type or favoured aspect. It says a lot for the adaptability of nature that some lived and even prospered. Anything that died I immediately replaced with some new

12

treasure, secretly glad of the space. If nothing else, my plants got plenty of water. I loved, and still do, to take a drink outside in the evenings and stand hose in hand till the whole place was awash. As the soil in our garden was naturally good, those plants which had lucked into a suitable spot flourished. The whole effect, while rather Lewis Carroll-like, was not unpleasing.

I blundered on thus for two or three years, getting some things right and quite a lot wrong. An ugly old fence needed a quick cover. Somewhere I read that *Cobaea scandens* was a good performer in this category. The common name Cathedral Bells sounded charming. And so it was for the first few months. As promised, it grew rapidly, covering not only the fence but the back gate as well—so effectively in fact that we couldn't open the gate and had to park the car in the street. Then most of the vine died, leaving large patches of dead leaves and stems inextricably entwined with the few remaining bits of greenery. From this time on, there was never less than three-quarters of the plant completely dead, presenting a melancholy picture in full view of the back windows. I compounded the original error by leaving it there instead of smartly ripping it out, I vaguely (and vainly) hoped for a rejuvenation and after all it had covered a great deal of the wooden paling fence which, I persuaded myself, was marginally worse. Perhaps not. Certainly, I would never plant a cobaea again.

Another of my early efforts which could not be rated a success was to buy (heaven knows where) and plant some tradescantia (Wandering Jew) as a ground cover. The enormity of this folly appals me even now. The plant is still with me, having infiltrated some pots that made the move with us. It survives the most scrupulous weeding, extreme drought, overplanting with ivy, concentrations of weedkiller that would polish off a hardwood forest and, quite possibly, nuclear annihilation. And I paid for it!

But despite all the failures and mistakes—and there were many more—there was also a great deal of pleasure. The annuals that I was so taken aback to discover had to be discarded, miraculously reappeared as tiny seedlings the next year. Once I had learned to recognize at least some of them, this was enormously gratifying. Even left exactly as they appeared—I am still unsure of the exact methodology of the practice referred to by the cognoscenti as 'pricking out' and had certainly never heard of it then—these small phoenixi produced a brave show at the appointed time. An assortment of ferns flourished in shady spots. Someone gave me a daphne and a bouvardia. They lived. A datura in the neighbour's garden hung its beautiful and deadly trumpets over the fence. I planted a jasmine which rapidly swarmed up the fence. The scents of these white beauties absolutely delighted me, especially during the evening watering ritual. The cherry tree gamely flowered round the sinkers. The cumquats fruited. I made brandied cumquats which tasted unspeakable but looked wonderful in the glass jars. A big pot of herbs, which I conscientiously used for cooking (everything) thrived by the back door. Order of a sort seemed to be settling over this other Eden.

In the Beginning

One of the immutable laws of gardening as I know it is that the slightest hint, the merest breath, of complacency such as is possible to detect in the preceding lines, activates some natural disaster or man-made calamity of cosmic proportions. As this was my first experience of this phenomenon, I was ill-prepared for it.

A severe drought hit Melbourne. This in itself is not unusual, occurring so regularly as to be routine. The real problem at this time was that the civic authorities whose business it was to arrange an adequate supply of water had spectacularly failed to do so. Draconian restrictions on the use of water were imposed; the citizens of Melbourne were exhorted to conserve water by any means possible. I certainly remember being urged to shower with a friend, though whether this was an official policy of our city fathers I cannot recall. As the summer progressed without rain, the use of a hose, even hand-held for an hour every second day, was completely forbidden. Melbourne, which the same municipal authorities had been pleased to designate 'The Garden City' became a city of bucket carriers.

It was a very long summer. The relaxing twilight spell with the hose became a stint of hard labour. The first thing to go was my drink—difficult to manage with a couple of sloshing buckets. I resented this very much at the time. I tried for a while to keep everything alive; I was out there until well after dark. So the annuals had to go. It was depressing in the extreme to see how little was left. The survivors looked more and more dessicated as the weeks went by. I continued to cart water around, tipping it on the iron hard ground around the roots.

Most of the water ran straight off and was wasted. At times it felt as if I was trying to irrigate the Sahara, a locale to which Victoria bore more that a passing resemblance at that time. It became fashionable to summon a team of dour individuals expert in sinking large holes in the lawn in the usually vain hope of locating usable water. Their advertising contained impressive claims of scientific technology and method. On one occasion I watched these wizards at work in a friend's garden. Their *modus operandi* was a little obscure, though I'm not at all sure that I didn't see a forked stick somewhere along the line. Great excitement ensued when they actually did find water. But the excitement didn't last long. 'Brackish!', a verdict delivered with a certain gloomy relish, dashed hopes of a rejuvenated oasis in the brown suburban wasteland. Discouraged, we didn't even try this solution. Soberer but sadder, I bucketed on.

Eventually, the rains came. No life-giving monsoon has ever been more welcome. All over Melbourne, gardeners disconsolately took stock. There were some casualties in my garden apart from the annuals. Most of the azaleas went, though one cultivar of a particularly virulent shade of magenta called 'Advent Bells' got through unscathed. This was a pity, as it looked even worse with the red Czar than had the 'Madame Auguste Haarens' all of which had swiftly succumbed. On the whole though, as the death of the Mesdames had removed the salmon-pink element from this colour grouping, it was probably a merciful release. Not surprisingly, the ferns also died, except for the fishbone which was merely slowed down a little in its campaign for world domination. It was surprising though, how much had survived. Lawns greened over as one watched; roses produced a magnificent thanksgiving of autumn blooms—the 'Queen Elizabeth' grew another foot in the excitement of the breaking of the drought. The hydrangeas, reduced to collections of dried sticks which looked completely dead, had merely lapsed into hibernation; with a little pruning, they sprang back into life the next year and flowered profusely the following season. The most unlikely survivors were the two camellias that had been forced into shallow scrapes among the roots of the Lillypilly. Against all odds they made it through and in fact are still alive today, somewhat bonsaied perhaps by the tree roots but fighting on. The camellia is clearly a very tough species.

My early complacency about my garden was severely shaken, but the gods of horticulture were still not appeased. We decided to do some minor renovations (our first) at the back of the house, innocently supposing this could be achieved without much disruption. Plans were drawn, builders engaged. New windows were going in, necessitating some removal of old walls. I moved all the pots to what I thought was a safe distance and, perhaps prompted by a dim memory of my father's tomatoes, inverted some wire hanging baskets and some old pots over all the small treasures that couldn't be easily shifted.

I was waiting for the workmen on the first morning. Yes, all of my shielded plants should be as right as rain. No worries at all, lady. We'll keep an eye on them. I went inside. I was (and still am) far too self-conscious to watch people working in case this might be interpreted as supervision. When the workers went off for lunch I went out to look. I couldn't believe it. I felt violated, shocked, assaulted. Plants and their pathetic covers had disappeared under tons of rubble. Pot plants, so carefully moved, were clearly the ideal spot for keeping your sledge hammer, pick, mattock, large thermos and spare pair of boots. Any plants which, like St Paul's during the Blitz, had escaped the avalanche of bricks and plaster were easily hobnailed to death. I couldn't bear the carnage; I fled the scene and sought refuge with a friend, demanding solace and a stiff drink.

Having now endured a number of bouts of building and renovation, I am tempted to conclude that, at the very least, building workers are schooled in total indifference to plants as part of their basic training in much the same way that doctors are conditioned to confront gashes and gore with cool detachment. At times I would have gone further and taken my bible oath that the mayhem was malicious. To be fair, this blind spot is not confined to workmen. One of the reasons that I now do most of the digging myself is that both my husband and my son, when summoned to wield the mattock, obliterate every living thing within a wide radius of the huge hole they hack out in a matter of minutes. Time and back-saving though this may be, the cost is too high; I would prefer to chip and scrape for hours than to have the area assume the appearance of a frequently used route for a herd of buffalo.

This is a reasonably accurate description of my back garden after the builders finally departed. But again it surprised me with its resilience. Fortunately, and entirely fortuitously, it was spring. The greening of the rubble was rapid and cheering.

Ground covers like needlepoint ivy sprang from entombment and spread with a will. The remains of shrubs, often only a single branch, produced green shoots in abundance. Admittedly this eventually led to some very curious shapes, but I leaned towards the sentimental in my approach in those days and regarded the new growth on the mangled remains as evidence of a gallant refusal to die in the face of overwhelming odds. Annuals re-appeared as seedlings in the crater and covered the scars in a matter of weeks.

The large new windows precipitated another buying frenzy: more pots, hanging baskets, even a highly ornate bird cage in which, for reasons which now escape me, I elected to grow ivy. By the following spring, not only had all signs of the upheaval disappeared but for the first time the garden began to look more settled and 'meant'; something to be enjoyed and even admired. That was when we sold the house.

BEGINNING
AGAIN

*W*e had been looking for a new house for some time. Our family had outgrown the small terrace; it was time to move on, though I regretted having to leave. I ranged far and wide around Melbourne, drawn by advertisements that regularly promised the house of my dreams but which never quite materialized. My husband was tolerant of this new hobby, but never entertained for a moment the notion of leaving the area. This led to a certain imbalance in our house-hunting activities; I had seen most of the vacant houses in Melbourne; he had looked at, and rejected, two.

Eventually I noticed a 'For Sale' sign on a high, dilapidated old fence within three blocks of where we were living. Nobody appeared to be about so, with some difficulty, I pushed the gate open and slipped in. Dream house it wasn't, although there was a certain nightmarish quality about it. It was clear why I'd had trouble with the gate. The front yard was edge-to-edge with waist-high grass and weeds. A couple of old apple trees leaned at drunken angles over the fence. Tangles of creepers, ancient overgrown shrubs and an unidentified vine with murderous thorns gave a Sleeping Beauty air to the house, which had obviously been empty for years. In an advanced state of decay, it was a single storied affair of dun-coloured cement, placed squarely in the middle of the block. It was built in a style which was not immediately —or even subsequently—identifiable as being of any particular architectural school or period. Or indeed, merit. A pair of heavy arches graced the front verandah. I tried to convince myself that these gave an Italianate look to the ruin, but I'm not sure I really believed it. A particularly feral-looking cat suddenly appeared through the long grass and glared balefully. The whole atmosphere was faintly menacing, and I retreated rather hurriedly.

We discussed the house that night, me with a noticeable lack of enthusiasm. It had one enormous plus; it was ninety metres from Melbourne's superb Botanic Gardens. We went back for an inspection.

The total picture was even worse than my first glimpse. The rooms were completely derelict; floorboards were missing, huge holes gaped in the ceilings and walls. A rabbit warren of dark little rooms, some with a single rusty tap and a pre-historic stove, suggested that at some time it had been a boarding house. We learned later that some years before, a very old and eccentric woman had lived in the house; the local children believed her to be a witch. She kept a myriad of cats and used to throw bottles over the fence at passers-by. The back yard was on at least three levels, as far as we could tell through the jungle of weeds, trees, a clothesline and a lean-to garage complete with vintage car. The back of the house tailed off into a structure which might have been a room or a shed. It was all quite horrendous. We bought it.

Shock set in soon afterwards, followed by grave doubts. Certainly the location of our new property was good; the rest was disastrous. Winter was closing in and on each visit the new house looked more like something out of 'Wuthering Heights'. An architect looked it over. 'What should we do?'

'Pull it down' was the sum total of his professional advice. It seemed like a good idea. I began visiting display homes which on the whole depressed me even more. We had got as far as a set of drawings for a new house when a friend who is also an architect phoned to say we were crazy; the old house was fine and just needed a little tidying up here and there. I am eternally grateful to this visionary friend. It was a long, slow haul and, like most renovations, a traumatizing experience. But we now have a solid comfortable old house of indeterminate style but some character and it suits us very well.

However, I do not intend to write at length about houses. While I had a certain input into the renovation and decoration, there was a large number of professionals involved in restoring the house to a liveable condition. They did their job very well. The garden, however, was largely my own work. We moved in, mowed down as much of the grass as we could and considered our quarter-acre estate.

The creation of a garden from a wilderness is a daunting task for a rank amateur such as I was; unfortunately, I wasn't daunted enough. The basic problem was not so much that I knew next to nothing, but that I didn't realize this at the time. Had I called in a professional then and there many problems that have plagued us ever since would have been avoided. But having from time to time produced a 'good show' in our first garden with some pots and annuals, I privately considered myself something of an expert. Occasionally friends even asked my advice. I'm ashamed to say that I gave it, probably with an air of grave authority. So I tackled the wilderness with all the confidence of that most dangerous of species, the possessors of a little knowledge.

At least I did make some attempt to start with the bones. The front fence had started to collapse as we signed the contract of sale and after six months of renovation had breathed its last before we moved in. So a firm of fence builders was called in to erect a brick wall. A high brick wall with a lightly bagged finish, the nearest we in the colonies can get to the mellowed-by-the-centuries appearance that photographs so well in English garden books. I liked the result and still do. So far, so good. However, trouble wasn't far away. The workmen asked me what I wanted done with the clay that had been excavated for the foundations. Coming from thirty centimetres or so below the surface it lay around in turgid grey lumps, about as harmless as Kryptonite. I now loathe the sight of it. Unfortunately, I didn't then recognize it for the menace it is. To me it was dirt, the stuff you put plants in. 'I guess you might as well leave it there' was my fateful reply. 'We have to have something to fill up the beds.' My words returned many times to haunt me.

A path from the front gate to the door was an urgent necessity. Somewhere I had read that it is a simple matter to set old bricks in a bed of sand and have small plants creeping charmingly between them. With me as artistic director, a pleasant youth who was somebody's second cousin set to work with great energy. Despite an illustrated magazine article on the subject and a lot of goodwill, somehow we didn't quite have the knack of it. A certain degree of rustic irregularity was acceptable, even desirable, but after a few months, our path was more of an obstacle course than an aid to anyone trying to make it to the front door. A number of guests with minor injuries, such as turned ankles, caused us to review our insurance and call in a qualified person to re-do the path. My tentative suggestion that we try the setting-in-loose-sand method one more time was met with such incredulity that I hastily withdrew it. I find it hard to challenge authority. In went the path on ten centimetres of solid concrete. At least it was no longer a health hazard.

The back yard was a trickier problem. It was not very big and half of it was occupied by a concrete drive and garage. Clotheslines were strung between several mournful specimens of that gloomy purple-leaved prunus. An enormous elm, apparently in the terminal phase of Dutch Elm disease, hung over the fence from the neighbour's garden. All the fences were bare wooden palings. The effect was hideous.

Then I got something right. I decided that we could park in the street as we had been doing since the cobaea had entered our lives. The garage and drive could go. Back came the builders to put in retaining walls. The purple prunus and the clothesline, which I found equally depressing, were ripped out. The lower level we filled, most laboriously, with truck-loads of soil. In a reckless surge of extravagance we invested in a number of long strips of lawn which were sold rolled up like a carpet. Voilà. A back garden. Well, at least it was a vast improvement.

Painting the Roses White

The greatest eyesore which remained was the fences. We had our new aged bricks at the front, but back and sides were defined by shabby wooden palings about one and a half metres high, the most common method for marking the limits of the Australian quarter-acre. Neighbours on both sides had apparently won the argument as to who was to have the wrong side of these dreary structures. Replacing them with something more aesthetically pleasing would have been prohibitively expensive. They had to be covered up. This I think is a very complex problem which I have never really resolved. It is also a very common problem in that everyone who lives in a city has fences of some sort, the great majority of which would be much better hidden from sight. Beautiful garden walls do not abound in the suburbs, at least in Australia. Also, in small gardens like mine, boundary fences tend to be close by, rather than on the far side of the spinney and across the ornamental lake. One sees them quite frequently. All of this means that when we who toil in the suburbs talk of covering fences, we actually mean covering rather than decorating. An expanse of rosy brick or Cotswold stone can stand a few months of winter exposure, wearing the bare stems of deciduous climbers with elegance whilst waiting for the adornment of roses or clematis flowers. Costwold stone being fairly thin on the ground in these parts, a more permanent cloak of foliage is highly desirable.

I have to say that I don't believe there is any such thing as a trouble-free fence cover. I decided to avoid the deciduous climbers for the reasons already discussed. Of the evergreens I tried, none was without its problems. In my very limited experience, evergreen climbers come in two varieties.

One group, after the first year or two, builds up huge matted tangles of deadwood underneath an increasingly sparse layer of green. Shades of the dreaded cobaea. Some *Jasminum polyanthum* and an evergreen honeysuckle that I planted also displayed this unfortunate habit. I knew that the prescribed cure, or preventative, is pruning. I did try this at one point with one of the jasmines. Approaching the thicket with determination, I tried to be selective in my cutting and thought that a few green strands were left clinging to life and the fence but these had obviously been severed somewhere deep in the maze since they quickly turned as brown as the rest. I do know, because I've read it a hundred times, that there is an appointed time to conduct this sort of surgery—that it must begin early in the life of the plant and that it must be carried out as regular as clockwork. Until such admirable routine becomes part of my life perhaps I would do better to avoid this type of climber altogether.

The other class of evergreen climbers in this rudimentary taxonomy I would describe as handsome rampers. The two star performers in this category are ficus and ivy. They have the big advantage of not having an off-season. Thus they are the best cover for the sort of fence in question—those of which it is best to catch not even a fleeting glimpse. The initially small-leaved *Ficus pumila* is a charming sight, clinging tightly to a wall or fence and climbing upwards in most attractive long vertical trails of tiny pink or green leaves. The same could be said for ivy, particularly the needlepoint varieties. Nothing could be more decorous than the small tendrils, tentatively creeping over bricks or trailing prettily over fences. Nothing could be more deceptive. Once established, these party manners vanish. My old faithful gardening bible did comment, mildly, of ficus that 'the small heart-shaped leaves are borne only by the young stems. Adult canes bear large leaves'. This is an inadequate warning for the alarming metamorphosis that transforms the attractive and even cover of dainty and restrained appearance into a rampant leviathan. At first I thought the new growth was another climber which had mysteriously materialized on my fence and was threatening to engulf the modest ficus I so admired. My rescue operation with the secateurs revealed the Jekyll and Hyde nature of the beast. It had to go.

Ivy also is subject to this uncalled-for mutation to a larger scale or a different form. Hedera comes in many shapes and sizes in my garden, all of them more or less unpredictable. About the only patch of green draping the fences when we arrived was an ancient straggle of the common large-leaved ivy on the back fence. Grateful for this single verdant patch, I left it there. It spread rapidly, gaining height (which was welcome) with the assistance of a few wires, and vast bulk which wasn't so desirable. Gathering strength over a number of years, it began to dispense with refinements like lobes on the leaves. The familiar five lobes were reduced to three on new leaves, and when the vine had gained undisputed control of most of the back garden it reverted to a primaeval form of huge leaves with no lobes at all. Nervously pecking at it with secateurs only goaded it to new surges of growth. The fence had long since disappeared. The ivy continued to gain height by some baffling bootstrap operation until it reached upwards of three metres. I began to fear for the fence. Surely a high wind would topple the ricketty old wooden planks burdened by that huge mass of greenery? We called in a qualified man. Scorning secateurs, he laid about him with axe and crosscut saw. I needn't have worried about the fence collapsing. The remains of the old palings will be there till Judgement Day, held up by tree trunks of the ivy. After the gardener had fought and hacked his way back towards the old fenceline, the vegetation he had felled was carted away by the truckload, and we eyed the twisted barricade of bare, arm-thick stems apprehensively. Could we live with this? Did we have a choice? Getting it out would require blasting. The question went into the too-hard basket.

One of the most welcome sights in my gardening life came a month or two later with the advent of spring. The ugly tangle of gross, amputated stems clothed themselves overnight in fresh green leaves. With the standard five lobes. Suddenly we had a beautiful, flat green wall which effectively screened out the house behind and provided a tranquil outlook from all of the back windows. Since the initial logging operation, a six-monthly shearing with electric clippers keeps chaos at bay. I think that this is as close as one can get to a trouble-free fence cover when real cover is needed, particularly if the clipping process begins before the ivy gets a taste of real power.

One of the side fences I also hid from sight under a curtain of ivy. In this instance, a friend gave us hundreds of cuttings of an attractive variety with curled, almost frilled leaves. The cuttings grew nobly, reaching the top of the fence within a few years. But again, some sort of regression to an ancestral form set in somewhere along the line. The mother plant at our friend's house to this day produces its leaves curled and frilled in the regulation manner. Nary a waver disturbs a leaf of mine—except on the new shoots for about five minutes in early spring—which now covers thirty metres of fence. I have had the same thing happen with the frilled-edge form of fish-bone fern which I think is called Boston fern. I have tried to establish this in shady spots to replace its ubiquitous cousin, the common fish-bone, to which it reverts the instant one's back is turned. Just why my garden has this curious atavistic quality which reverses the normal processes of evolution I have yet to discover.

On the remaining side of our rectangle I decided to try Potato Vine (*Solanum jasminoides*) as a beautifying veil. This useful if ubiquitous creeper grows and flowers with great enthusiasm and generosity. Given favourable conditions, the jasmine-like foliage and simple white flowers are an attractive sight for most months of the year. I feel very strongly that this is a quality of paramount importance in small gardens and should receive more attention from garden writers. Indeed, after many years of learning a limited amount the hard way, I would still very much appreciate a simplified chart which indicates clearly the number of months of the year during which plants are an asset in the garden rather than a liability. Something like:

	Looks Good	*Flowers*	*Looks Terrible*
Solanum	11 months	10 months	Doesn't
Clematis	5 months	2 weeks	7 months
Ivy	12 months	N/A	Doesn't
Cobaea	Doesn't	Half-heartedly	12 months

This sort of chart, particularly with the 'Looks Terrible' column, would be invaluable in the selection of plants for the small garden where every centimetre is precious and each plant is seen frequently if not constantly. I would also find most helpful the addition of another column entitled 'Do Not Use If . . .'. The entry in this column for Potato Vine might read 'The supporting fence is shaded except for the very top', which is an accurate description of the long side fence I wanted the creepers to cover. Without the benefit of such a directive, I planted the vines the entire length of the fence. Years later, this side boundary remained a desolate sight, the wooden palings festooned with a thicket of bare stems. Right at the top, a fringe of leaves and flowers made a brief appearance before cascading triumphantly down the other side, a mass of lush foliage and white blossom which cheered the neighbours enormously. The infuriating thing about making a mistake in choosing fence covers is that, in most cases, the whole process is so slow. Years pass, youth vanishes, dynasties rise and fall as creepers inch upwards and thicken into a solid bulwark against the world or at least the block of flats next door. Starting again from scratch equates with surveying a completed pyramid and deciding 'A little to the left, I think'. Nonetheless, this is what I have decided to do on the solanum-clad fence. Once again, hundreds of ivy cuttings are currently looking pathetic at the foot of the gaunt palings. I hope I've got it right this time.

It will be clear from the foregoing that I favour ivy in some form as a desirable part of the bones of a small garden. It seems to me the most satisfactory substitute for the backdrop of evergreen hedges which appears to be standard issue in English and European gardens. Splendid as these ramparts of yew and cypress undoubtedly are, they are somewhat impractical for a quarter-acre block since they would probably meet in the middle, so we must be content with an evergreen of more modest girth. Ivy can be kept to a few centimetres of thickness with regular trimming and still look solidly green, so it gets my vote for the outer fences. It must be admitted, though, that there are drawbacks. It is very difficult to confine ivy to the fence itself.

Most suburban gardens have the bulk of the planting in beds around the fenceline, as indeed did mine. Ivy planted to cover the fence occupies these beds as a matter of course, and it takes a real fighter to successfully compete with the green tide. Some surprising plants turn out to be made of stern stuff. One small azalea which I have never really liked continues to flower grimly every year though well nigh submerged. Such grittiness impresses me; I can't quite bring myself to pull it out, sentimental though this may be. But on the whole, if you opt for one of the evergreen rampers on the fences, it will triumph in the end. Certainly all will be green and beautiful, but perhaps a trifle monotonous. One possible solution is potted plants. I was most inspired by the sight of potted citrus in an Italian garden I visited years ago. Large terracotta pots stood at intervals along a high ivy clad wall. Each contained a thriving orange tree covered in fruit. The oranges positively glowed against the dark green background. Very Heironymous Bosch. I have found that similarly striking effects can be achieved with potted roses, geraniums, lilies, bulbs or indeed any flowering or fruiting plant which can be induced to grow in a container. At the moment I have a flat bowl of small polyanthus standing on a low table against my back ivy wall. Being winter, there is little else in flower. The wall is three metres high. The polyanthus are 10 centimetres. They are seen instantly, as if spotlighted.

However, a cautionary note should be sounded about using ivy near the house. My attempts to use needlepoint ivy as a ground cover in beds which adjoined the house proved disastrous. The variety I got hold of turned out to be the self-clinging type which snaked up the house walls, looking very pretty as it insinuated itself into window frames, gutters and eventually the slates on the roof. With great reluctance, the decision was taken to remove it while we still had some shelter from the elements. That was the easy part. Getting it out was another matter. The clinging apparatus of this creeper would not disgrace a limpet mine. Ripping the long strands from the walls left a pattern of fibrous roots which called to mind Aboriginal cave paintings. When the house was eventually repainted a very determined and thorough painter tried all the tricks of his trade to remove the remains, by then years old, but in the end he admitted defeat and painted over them. Possibly I was unlucky in my choice of variety in this case, but I am now very nervous about allowing ivy direct access to my house.

Aside from covering the fences, a great deal of planting had to be done at the outset. We had very few trees, apart from the obligatory Lillypilly or two. One of the ancient apple trees we inherited had fallen into the hole dug for the new front fence. It's a great pity the other one didn't go in as well, as it turned out to be rotten right through but I was thrilled it had survived to hang its apples over the brick wall, so it stayed. An alder (Alnus) was planted, unfortunately without a stake, to replace the casualty. It soon developed a 45 degree lean away from the prevailing wind, and loomed threateningly at passers-by in the street, forcing them into the road to pass. A neighbour gave me a large variegated pittosporum, which I hated. He was a charming old man who presented the tree with some ceremony, so I felt obliged to plant the wretched thing on the side fence where he could see it. It surprised me very much by looking good, lightening what was a rather gloomy walkway. I put a slender liquidambar sapling (*Liquidambar styrasiflua*) in a very cramped corner next to the path. This now regularly disrupts telephone contact with the outside world as it soars past the wires. I outdid myself, however, in my choice of trees for the back fence. As space was at a premium I thought we needed a bit of height without excessive bulk. So I put in four lemon-scented gums (*Eucalyptus citriodora*) right on the fence line and actually set one into some steps which led down to the back lane. The trees must now

be 20 metres tall, waving far above the ivy and the neigh-
bouring house which they were intended to screen. Inside the
fence, the remains of the steps decorate the roots. Outside,
the brick retaining wall bulges outward, plainly on the verge
of bursting asunder. A neighbour every evening parks his small
car right next to the biggest bulge. I do wish he wouldn't.
The whole thing may be swept away or buried in the night.
Several times we have decided to have the gums removed.
This decision is usually reached during that season in which
they shed every centimetre of their bark, covering everything
in sight with great grey flakes with all the visual appeal of
dandruff. Add to that a light rain of branches, twigs and leaves
which is a daily feature regardless of season and it will be plain
why the treelopper's phone number is looked up fairly
regularly. Then I look at the silver trunks and, by craning
upwards, at the graceful grey-green foliage, put away the
telephone book and get out the rake. What we'll do when
the wall bursts I'm not quite sure. I just hope it's during
working hours.

With trees planted, my garden construction had at last reached
the stage of considering flowering plants which, as far as I
was concerned, was what it was all about. At this opportune
moment a friend who was re-building offered me some mature
camellias and azaleas. I leapt at the offer. The services of their
rather intimidating German gardener were proffered for a day
to shift the quite large plants. I leapt with even greater alacrity
at this offer. He called to discuss the project and survey the

intended home for his plants. Diffidently I indicated the bed adjoining the front fence which, even to my eyes, looked less than ideal. Grass and weeds sprouted wherever they could scrabble a foothold between the great lumps of clay which had set like concrete. In fact, they were indistinguishable from the great lumps of concrete the builders had left behind in goodly measure. The gardener stared stonyfaced at this prospect. The silent type, he nevertheless contrived to radiate incredulity and disapproval. Finally, with an air of heroic restraint, he settled for a simple instruction: 'That has to go'. With which he left to begin excavating the plants.

Needless to say, no one else was around. Seizing a pick and a wheelbarrow, I began a frenzied attack on the mullock-heap, it having been made clear to me that time was of the essence in this delicate operation. Load after load of concrete and clay was rushed around and dumped in the furthest back corner of the garden. (We eventually built a shed over it— it seemed the simplest solution). By the time my forbidding friend arrived back with a truckload of plants swathed in hessian, it was at least possible to make a depression in the ground to receive them.

The gardener worked in grim silence. He appeared to favour a certain precision in his plantings, as the shrubs went in at exactly equal intervals in a straight line along the front fence and down the sides. I offered no resistance. For some reason I found myself a bit tired which seemed to take the edge off my interest in proceedings. With a final stern exhortation not to let the plants dry out under any circumstances, he departed at the end of the day looking deeply pessimistic about their chances. Unnecessarily, as it turned out. They all survived. One or two of the camellias were quite pretty, though I never could identify any of them. However, the rest tended to have harsh pink flowers of a muddled and undistinguished form. The foliage always looked as if the bushes could not forgive the upheaval; limp and inclined to yellow. The azaleas, when they came into flower, proved to be a mixture of red, magenta, orange and mauve varieties, positioned with unerring accuracy to effect the most vicious clashes. This time I did notice that the whole effect was less than harmonious. Something had to be done to separate the warring elements.

At this time, tree ferns (*Dicksonia* spp.) were in vogue. Never one to swim against the tide, I decided these were just the thing to complement my assorted shrubs. These strange and ancient giant ferns were ripped by the thousand from the shady gullies in the bushland where they had been growing very slowly and peacefully for centuries. Head and feet chopped off, the torsos were stacked in corners of nurseries to be purchased by the metre. Five dollars per half metre, one dollar for a year's growth. Carted home in the boot, they were stuck upright in the ground like hairy totem poles, usually right out in the open, facing north where they could give a good show. Some had the good sense to die at once. Many gamely unfurled their pale green fronds to be barbecued in January temperatures of 40 degrees. This was the fate of some of the ferns I bought, but others lucked into the shady side bed and in fact did well.

This side walkway I came to regard as the most successful part of my garden. It was a most curious and catholic mixture.

The brick path from the front gate ran down the middle, with two long narrow beds on either side. It was deeply shaded by the tall house next door and three golden ashes. In addition to the transplanted camellias and the tree ferns, I put in three 'E.G. Waterhouse' camellias next to the house. These grew prodigiously, reaching the eaves in a very few years. They are vigorous Williamsii hybrids with small pointed dark green leaves and clear pale pink semi-double flowers which looked very good against the pink wall of the house. I wish I'd heard of the art of espalier then, but the bushes still look good as they are, even if we do have to chop the tops off every so often as they reach for the sky. In front of these I planted several *Nandina domestica* (alternatively called sacred bamboo—a fairly loose translation I've always thought) which gave a pleasantly lush effect. On the other side of the path went a number of *Rhododendron* 'Pink Pearl'. The only flowers these have ever borne have been so far above my head that I've never actually seen one. Not a good choice for a cramped situation.

The rest of the planting in these beds could be grouped under the general heading of 'house escapes'. I had, like many others at this time, built up a considerable indoor plant collection with a distinctly Victorian flavour. Kentia palms were the *pièces de resistance* of this collection which also featured ferns, parlour palms, a fan palm, an umbrella plant or two and the wonderfully named fatshedera, which looks like a gross form of ivy. There were also two Bangalow palms which looked a perfectly manageable size in their pots. What I didn't realize is that these were very juvenile specimens of a very adult-sized palm tree. This collection had lived indoors in the old house, battling, and frequently losing, against the central heating. The survivors had made the move with us, and for a time continued their existence as house plants. Then the wheel of fashion turned; Victoriana was out, *Ficus benjamina* became *de rigueur*.

It was at once clear to me that this was indeed a superior plant in every way. We soon had several fine and expensive specimens installed in the house in large cane baskets, along with flowering orchids. This was my tropical rain forest period. But I couldn't quite bring myself to completely discard the ousted favourites. They looked quite attractive dotted among the tree ferns and camellias in the side beds, so I dug them into the ground. As a finishing touch to the walkway, we hung staghorn (*Platycerium grande*) and elkhorn (*P. bifurcatum*) ferns at regular intervals along the high trellis that topped the fence. These plants are most aptly named. They are commonly mounted on boards and hung from trees or fences in exactly the same manner as hunting trophies and indeed look very similar. The principal difference is that the ferns are predators rather than prey, having the ability to kill a large tree if allowed to completely encircle the trunk. Even on a fence they must be regularly appeased with banana skins stuffed down their throats. Why I felt that a line of these parasites was an ornament to my fence I can't imagine. Unless it could have been that they were very fashionable at the time.

Well satisfied with my efforts, I proceeded to totally neglect the whole area for years. The demands of small children distracted me somewhat from dilettante activities like watering and weeding. It was survival of the fittest out there. Some of the survivors proved to be very fit indeed. Just how fit was borne in upon me one very wet day when we were awaiting the arrival of friends. Confused cries reached our ears. 'My God, it's like bloody Sumatra!' Calls for machetes and guides were heard. The friends finally got to the rarely used front door soaked to the skin and understandably a little irritated. Contrite, I inspected the path next day. To say it was overgrown is to understate the case by quite a long shot. The Kentia palms were three metres tall and the Bangalows looked positively Somerset Maugham. One could make out clusters of dates or perhaps small coconuts swaying far above the roof. The tree ferns had not increased much in height but had made up for it by throwing huge fronds across the path, hiding it from view. The tops of the camellias emerged from sizeable sacred groves of nandina. At a lower level, fatshedera sprawled exuberantly around the fronds of fan and parlour palms. The stags and elks had devoured their boards and made considerable inroads on the fence. Ivy encroached on everything. The effect was roughly that of an old Tarzan movie set. It was at this point that we decided that we really had to have a proper gardener to come in for an hour or two a week just to keep the show on the road. Or off the path. A very calm and pleasant man was found who cut an access tunnel without the severe slashing and chopping that I hated. He still comes every fortnight for two or three hours which is very helpful, but how I wish it was more often.

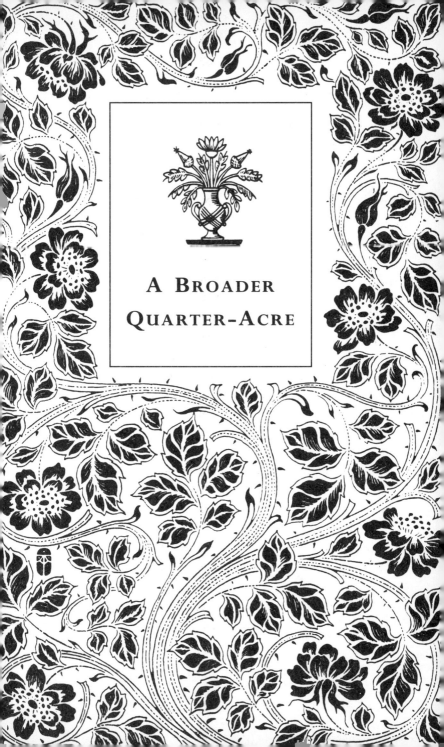

A BROADER
QUARTER-ACRE

*S*ome years after we moved in, we were able to acquire an extra strip of land about eight metres wide running the length of our block. This was a great piece of luck and the cause of much rejoicing. It enabled us to extend the house to include more distant quarters for the children, a move which was equally appreciated by all parties. I was eventually persuaded on the grounds of cost to drop plans for a portcullis and a moat between the old and new sections. Another bout of building began.

Our new strip of real estate did come with a number of assorted shrubs and trees, but they almost all disappeared under the now familiar cataclysm of concrete, tradespeople, trucks *et al* which moved in for the next six months. So the sole legacy from the old garden next door was the huge and moribund elm which until now had been on the other side of the fence. Now it was our responsibility. It was certainly a mixed blessing. Definitely on the debit side was its appearance. Although age and sheer size conferred a certain haggard grandeur, the battle-scarred veteran of a thousand storms was anything but a picture of grace and symmetry. Every one of its main branches had at some time been broken and ended in a jagged stump. Large splits in the main trunk threatened to tear the tree asunder. In addition, the elm was now at the end of the straight row of lemon-scented gums across the back of the block. The fence between them had made it clear that this odd mixture was not my doing, but with the fence gone it looked decidedly eccentric. A further major setback for the tree was looming in that we wanted to put a swimming pool at its feet—the only available space—entailing much excavation of the root area. Much agonizing ensued. Would it die? Would it drop a branch on some hapless swimmer? Should we take it out now while we still could? Of course we didn't do anything of the sort, though it was clearly the logical course to follow. The sheer size of the thing made its assassination seem a crime of some enormity. The final plan involved a pool of bizarre shape and little practical use, unless you like to swim round corners, which skirted round the roots as much as possible. A tree surgeon was summoned, an important person who spent some days aloft sawing, painting, bracing and filling—operations which are evidently considerably more difficult and expensive to perform than brain surgery. Trimmed, medicated, held together with bolts and chains, the old warrior lived to fight another day, though we still hold our breath every spring waiting for the first signs of green. I refuse to think about what we'll do if it dies; the only option that immediately suggests itself is to sell the house the next winter.

It was the tree surgeon who suggested, eyeing the lunar landscape left by the builders and the pool contractors, that a little professional help in planning the garden's beautification would not go amiss. I thought this an excellent idea. A friend of the tree surgeon's arrived promptly. His card announced him to be a landscape designer. I had never met one before. Impressed as always by expertise in an unfamiliar field, I asked for no references and ventured little enquiry as to his favoured style. Nor did it occur to me to ask to see examples of his work. I followed him around the site, nodding respectfully and mendaciously to indicate understanding of technical terms like scoria, sleepers and aggie pipes. Mercifully I had seen pebble mix before, so was able to veto its use as a pool surround and substitute my brick pavers. For the rest, he had *carte blanche*.

It soon became clear that he was of the school which favoured the simple approach to garden design. Obviously sensitive to the perils of introducing too many elements to confuse the eye, he confined himself to just two: railway sleepers and grevillea. With the odd rock as an accent (or should that be dot?). The use of a single genus (even if it had to be grevillea) need not have been monotonous—I have discovered since that there is an enormous range of shapes and sizes of these versatile plants. This man preferred to stick to the lowish extra prickly varieties for all situations, even at the foot of a stretch of high brick wall acquired with our new land. Possibly he was striving, in the best traditions of his profession, for an overall effect of restful tranquillity or classical simplicity. If so, he didn't quite pull it off. 'Boring' comes closer to describing the general ambience after he had finished and departed. Disappointed with the fruits of these expert labours, I reminded myself of the often salutary effects of the passage of time and tackled the next project alone.

Building an extension along the side of a house poses the obvious problem of getting natural light into the rooms which become the centre of the building. The problem was most acute for the main bedroom. Skylights were considered, but for a devout claustrophobic like myself these were totally inadequate. So a courtyard opening off the bedroom was incorporated into the design. I was thrilled. I should perhaps explain here that I have the great good fortune to travel to Italy from time to time on business trips with my husband. The influence of this most beautiful of countries on my thinking about house and garden has been profound. So of course I was delighted to have a courtyard. One of these trips coincided with the building of our extensions. Wandering around the Vatican on the obligatory hunt for the Sistine Chapel, I happened upon the Belvedere Courtyard. It is stunningly beautiful. It is also immense, the scene of jousts and pageants, of whole convocations of cardinals. My courtyard is two-and-a-half metres by three-and-a-half metres. It will surprise no one to learn that this anomaly didn't deter me in the least. I had my model.

In the back streets of Florence I found a small dark antique shop where I bought a marble fountain. It was very cheap as the owner classified it as modern trash, no more than two hundred years old. Elated with this shrewd buying, we arranged for it to be shipped home for little more than the cost of its weight in gold. It was installed in a shallow hexagonal pool in the centre of the courtyard which was paved with pale terracotta tiles. We had some Water in the Garden. Readers of the literature of garden design will be aware that water is mandatory in any garden worthy of the name. While it sounds charming in the abstract, the practicalities are a minefield for the unwary. There is no getting around the fact that water, unless it is constantly in fairly violent motion, very soon becomes very unattractive indeed. Pumps can be installed, but it is dauntingly expensive to run a pump continuously. Most people opt for swtiching it on when it is desired to impress someone. This is not nearly enough to discourage the green slime. Consequently, water features in many suburban gardens tend to the opaque khaki rather than the limpid clear end of the aqueous spectrum. A friend who has a small, supposedly decorative pool has run the entire gamut of cures recommended by various experts for turbid waters: oxygenating plants, snails and water fleas have all been cast into the deep. None has had the slightest discernible effect on the clarity of the water. The pond continues to look like a remnant of the primordial swamp, surely a doubtful asset in a small garden.

Another method of incorporating the essential H_2O was urged upon us recently in a magazine article I happened to read. Nothing is more tranquil and soothing to the spirit, the reader was assured, than a simple stone bowl of clear water strategically positioned in the herb garden. The picture did indeed appear just so. It was the thought of the herculean task of emptying and refilling the stone bowl to ensure continued clarity that worried me a little. Perhaps a vigorous jet from the hose would do the trick, though the bowl preferred as a model seemed a very deep and solid one.

What I wanted was a fountain like those in the streets and

piazzas of Rome; no fish, no waterlilies or weeds, just beautiful clear water. How the Italians manage it I'm not sure, but I opted for chemical control. Household bleach is tipped into the bowl whenever the green slime strikes. It seems to work quite well, though birds fly away from a drink looking thoughtful.

I have experimented with many plants in my courtyard. Cumquats in pots looked very good standing around the fountain, but failed to thrive. The courtyard is so small that for most of it direct sunlight is limited to an hour or two a day. In each corner, four tiles were left out and small mandarin trees planted. These grew rapidly despite limited sunlight and when in peak form looked marvellous with the terracotta tiles and pink walls. But an unsightly problem was that the mandarins fought upwards towards the light and quickly became leggy and bare at the bottom. In an effort to rectify this I put in a lot of minute box plants round the edges of the square holes. Gazing far into the future, I could see neatly clipped little formal hedges hiding the legs of the mandarins very well. You need your fair share of vision to be a gardener.

Two *Ficus benjamina* (house escapees; I had emerged from the indoor tropical rain forest era) in pots were lushly green most of the time although every now and again after a cold spell they unnerved me by dropping every single leaf and giving a very convincing impression of two dead trees. Time after time, though, they miraculously contrived to produce thick new foliage just as the last trump was sounding.

I was very pleased with the walls of my courtyard. A display

A Broader Quarter-Acre

at a garden show of pots blooming on a wall caught my eye some years ago. They were suspended by a device called a pot ring, an unobtrusive metal ring which fits under the rim of a pot and hooks into an attachment plugged into the wall. Vertical rows of four squat terracotta pots were fixed to three walls of the courtyard. I tried various annuals in them, always the same variety in all twelve pots. Probably the most successful was the lobelia 'Cambridge Blue', though keeping them watered in summer was a full time job. If all requirements were met, the lobelia cascaded down the walls in a blue wave. Babylonian, perhaps? To round out the historical pot pourri, the fourth wall bears a terracotta mask which is undoubtedly one of the Greek Furies. All this in two-and-a-half metres by three-and-a-half metres. Surprisingly, it all looked quite harmonious. Certainly when completed I thought it an improvement on the monoculture in the back garden. It is unfortunate that this whole scheme eventually fell into the 'best-laid-plans' category. One of the mandarins received many hours of sunlight daily and grew enormous. Another got almost none and died. The box hedges never got past the scruffy stage and harboured battalions of snails. Watering the suspended pots became so onerous that early retirement looked a distinct possiblity, either for me or the pots. The current arrangement is definitely the last. I think. The mandarins have been replaced by *Ficus hillii*. These are relatively inexpensive and splendidly sturdy members of the fig family which take readily to standardizing. Having reluctantly concluded that there was little I could do about the habits of the sun, I bought one tree which was already taller than the others, opting for a bit of artistic asymmetry. The pots and the box were relocated. The Greek Fury rather crossly contemplates this retreat from the vision splendid, but I'm not sure that it's not a relief to have a little less busyness in what is really a very small space.

THE
DARK AGE

*I*n this roughly chronological account of the evolution of a small garden there now follows a decade when very little happened at all. Intoxicated by the feeling of liberation, albeit from willing bondage, when my youngest child started school, I rushed headlong back to the groves of academe— though in my case it was a very lowly grove; more of a shrubbery really. In hindsight, I rushed too soon and with very little thought of where it would lead. At the time, I just knew it was wonderful to set off with a purpose and a destination every morning and exhilarating to feel the mind creak painfully into gear. My erratic attention and enthusiasm were channelled into my new hobby (I called it career) with a fanatical zeal quite uknown in my earlier brushes with learning. Lectures took precedence over frivolities like meals, exams disrupted holidays, school sports days were spent in a library. A mere pass was unthinkable, anything less than the highest honour unacceptable, causing deep depression and filthy moods, the brunt of which was borne by my long-suffering family. Why and how they put up with all this ego-tripping nonsense I don't know, but they did, and I'm very grateful to them.

During this time when I diligently, indeed feverishly, sought the glittering prizes, the garden was kept from total reversion to the wild by the brief fortnightly visit of the gardener who singlehandedly fought a gallant holding action. Very occasionally in spring something stirred deep within and

I was moved to a little desultory planting. A row of 'Iceberg' roses went in along the sunny fence in the front garden. Two Japanese plum trees were planted at the foot of the high brick wall in the back garden. With a hazy idea of espaliering, I simply cut off any branch which grew forward. This has produced two half trees rather than shapely trained speci-mens, but they look pretty flowering against the wall or laden with fruit. These plums are very undemanding trees, getting by without the elaborate spraying programme that seems to be essential for the fussier peaches and nectarines. Any fruit that can be salvaged from the birds makes very good eating being juicy and dark-red.

I enjoyed the notion of harvesting something from my own garden, so I planted a fruiting grape to grow over a pergola at the back of the house. This was a mistake. Far from being the haven of green and dappled shade I had envisaged, the back terrace in late summer resembled an overcrowded wildlife enclosure. Birds and possums nightly held Baccha-nalian revels of such epic proportions that the end results, so to speak, were disastrous. Anyone rashly venturing out in the morning found himself knee-deep in guano. In desperation, I bought some bird nets of fine black mesh and with some difficulty draped them over the whole vine. The birds simply flew in and ate their fill from underneath. The nets did seem to discourage the possums, though, so they remained in place. Then I arrived home one day to find my daughter, tears streaming down her face, precariously bal-anced on a ladder trying to free an enmeshed bird with a pair of nail scissors. A confused scene ensued. The bird's role consisted of spirited attempts to blind us both as we swayed about on the ladder. My daughter, a passionate animal lover, alternately made soothing noises at the wretched thing and hurled imprecations at me as a murderer and assassin. The bird was finally cut free from the net and hurtled to the ground where it began a demented dashing about, obviously unable to fly. A mad pursuit followed to the accompaniment of mounting hysteria from at least two of the cast. Cornered at last, the bird was freed of the remaining strands of netting at no greater cost than a couple of Samaritan fingers slashed to the bone. Although the bird had escaped apparently without injury, the point was made quite forcefully to me that the nets had to go. So now every summer, just before the grapes ripen, I drag out a large rubbish bin and cut every bunch off the vine. I can see why most people plant the ornamental variety.

❧

Another ill-considered acquisition was the black bamboo. I don't remember how I arrived at the conviction that life in inner city Melbourne would be immeasurably improved with the addition of a few stands of this exotic grass. Perhaps the image of bloody Sumatra had subconsciously appealed to me. At this time, in the mid-seventies, the jungle look was the *dernier cri*; philodendrons and banana palms strove to look tropical instead of frostbitten around Melbourne swimming pools, strelizias and ginger lilies lined front paths, solar topees were issued at the gate. In such a milieu, a clump or two of this species of bamboo with its black lacquered stems and pale green foliage would have been a *coup de théâtre*. Which is probably what inspired me to pay a great deal for half a dozen miserable single stalks in old tins which were unearthed in the corner of an obscure nursery and duly planted along a side fence. They appeared to approve of the change. The forlorn stalks rapidly thickened into very respectable clumps which, when I noticed them at all, pleased me very much.

It was the gardener who pointed out a year or two later that he was mowing the tops off spikes of bamboo that were appearing in the lawn six metres or more away from the parent clumps. This I found faintly alarming. He also suggested that I look at the black bamboo in the fernery in the Botanic Gardens. Pleased to hear there was a mature colony so close to hand, I walked down there. I couldn't immediately identify any black bamboo, so sought help from one of the staff. The scale of my search had been wrong. A Lilliputian figure in the dim forest, I thoughtfully contemplated the Amazonian trunks of the grass I had planted. I couldn't see the tops; they were obscured by low cloud. Something clearly had to be done quite quickly on the home front.

The gardener, obliging man that he is, thought there was a solution. He dug up the clumps, a mighty task in itself, and I bought some massive concrete tubs. With the bottoms knocked out, they were sunk in the ground and the clumps of bamboo divided and replanted in them. This worked well for a while. We got no more satellite spikes appearing in the lawn and the divided clumps grew well in their concrete prison. But after several years of neglect, the plants started to look tatty and underfed, having outgrown the containers, and the roots had jumped over the edge on the surface and were making a determined bid for freedom. I don't know that there is a safe and satisfactory way of growing the larger species of bamboo in a small garden unless one is willing to spend a lot of time and work on the project. If pots are used to confine the roots, and I think they almost must be, then it is necessary to lift, divide and replant at regular intervals, probably every two or three years. Not a job for the faint-hearted.

Apart from such occasional spasms of ineffectual activity, during this era the garden was simply left to get on with it. And it looked like it. At times, its feral condition attracted even my husband's attention, usually when he got soaked to the skin trying to fetch the newspaper from the letter-box after overnight rain. Not that he ever did anything about it himself, but a spate of directives would be issued to the unfortunate gardener on the all-too-rare occasions when he appeared. 'Spate' is perhaps pitching it a bit strong; there were only two directives really: 'Cut everything back' and 'Get rid of that damned acanthus'. Just why this blameless plant has attracted such implacable animosity from my spouse I am not sure. But attract it it certainly has. He seems convinced that every living thing on the property is at risk while any shred of acanthus remains. I must have remarked at some point that it was difficult to eradicate when I found that it will shoot again from the smallest piece of root. Triffids may even have been mentioned. No acanthus fancier myself in the early days, I was converted when I learned that

(a) the Greeks so admired its leaves that they sculpted them on the capitals of a fair percentage of their columns, and (b) in the Middle Ages it was known as Bear's Breeches. Any plant that can combine classical and medieval elements in its lineage can't be all bad, and I began to regard acanthus with a more kindly eye. Too late; my earlier warning had taken firm root. Only constant vigilance on the part of the paterfamilias would prevent a complete acanthus takeover. The acanthus-spotting tours of the garden continue to this day. No truffle has been more keenly sought. It says a lot for the plant's resilience that the triumphant cry of discovery is still heard from time to time.

The gardening contributions of the other family members, then, remained largely negative. Visiting children, ably led by my son, regularly denuded the cumquats of fruit to provide ammunition for a friendly war or two in the garden. I have never yet encountered a child who on the way past could resist stripping the leaves from the stalks of fish-bone fern in one smooth motion. As they passed quite frequently during these years, it soon looked as if the retreating armies had adopted a rigorous scorched-earth policy.

The potted plants probably suffered the most during this period, given that they need a lot of attention to do their best. I remember one exasperated friend with a more stable horticultural passion than mine asking why on earth I didn't stir myself sufficiently to pull a few of the larger weeds out of the pots and try to get some water into the iron-hard soil in them. Conscience-stricken, I did so once then promptly forgot them again. It is incredible that any of the potted plants survived at all but many, like the cumquats, proved to be doughty fighters. Melbourne does have adequate rainfall for most years for plants in the ground, but I find that pots can stay dry even after quite heavy rain; dense bushes like citrus act as very effective umbrellas. I now spend a lot of time watering pots which makes the survival of those original specimens even more mystifying. They do look considerably better now—there was a very lean and hungry look about them in the Years of the Mind.

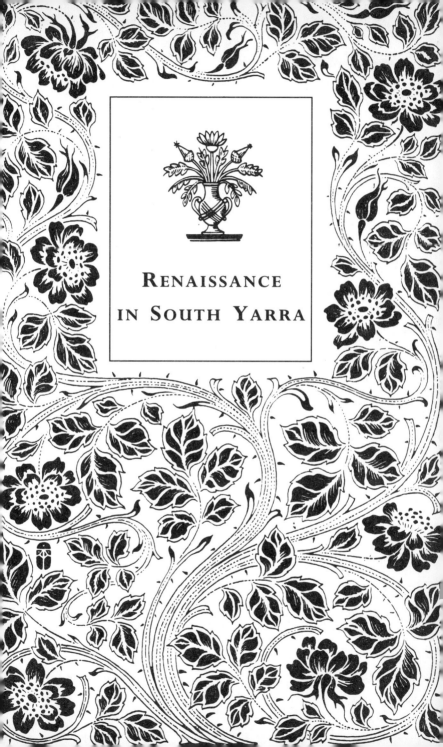

RENAISSANCE
IN SOUTH YARRA

*E*ventually and inevitably, and not a moment too soon for my family, the fires of zealotry began to die down. The Holy Grail of high academic honours faded back to its only possible position for me—unattainable. Like someone recovering from a long illness, I gradually resumed old interests like seeing friends, playing tennis, talking to the children. And gardening. But this time there was a difference. The years of study had, if nothing else, entrenched the habit of seeking to remedy ignorance by consulting the written word of experts. Reading books, if you like. Until now, my horticultural research had consisted of the occasional dip into 'Women's Weekly Gardening In Colour' and 'Yates Garden Guide', sterling publications both and very sound on the cultivation of brassicas and the layering of carnations, but a little light on inspirational design. With the present of a copy of Georgina Masson's 'Italian Gardens', then in small paperback form, some blessed if forgotten benefactor opened up the vast and varied treasure trove of garden literature.

I must admit at once that my reading in this field was then, and remains, firmly in the popular category. Technical publications like learned monographs on the family *Scrophalariaceae* I avoid altogether, and even mildly erudite prose such as that in Ms Masson's excellent book brings on a glazing of the eyes and a tendency to dwell on the pictures. Sharply edited anthologies of the best garden writers found great favour, as did coffee table volumes with titles like 'An

Illustrated History of the Garden—216 Colour Plates'. It was into such relatively easy waters that I now plunged with enthusiasm.

It was not long before these intoxicating visions of real gardens engendered a profound dissatisfaction with what I saw from every window whenever I lifted my eyes from the colour plates. The contrast was marked to say the least. The front garden was a sloping, dispirited rectangle of patchy, spongey buffalo grass surrounded by narrow beds containing sullen, clay-bound camellias, burnt tree ferns, a decaying apple tree and the leaning alder. The only plants which were thriving were an exuberant thicket of wandering jew and the indestructible 'Icebergs'. The side walkway looked parched and neglected as the three ash trees were now huge and taking all available water and nourishment. The back garden was as bland and boring as ever. My little piece of Vatican was the only remotely pleasing sight. The rest had to be drastically revamped. But how? For the first time I gave some consideration to the vexed question of style. Until this turning point, my approach had been overwhelmingly and confusedly that of a plantsman. It could perhaps be characterized as the 'Lost Horizon' approach. Years ago I happened to see a film of that name. I can only assume that I was trapped on a plane; it was awesomely bad. One of the highlights was the chance discovery by a motley group of misfits, led by an embarrassed Peter Finch, of a secret valley somewhere in the endless snows of the Himalayas. Changes in the micro-climate must be quite marked in those parts. The lushest of tropical greens, the most brilliant of rainbow-hued flowers greeted the

understandably startled travellers as they staggered through
the frozen pass. The usual arrangement of four seasons had
been waived by some Hollywood sorcerer. Roses, winter
bulbs, hydrangeas, lilies, blossom trees, dahlias and orchids
rioted in full bloom all over the celluloid Shrangri-La. It was
exactly the vision of Paradise I had been seeking all my
gardening life. Every visit to a nursery resulted in the purchase
of a pot of whatever was in full bloom all the time and
cunningly positioned to attract maximum attention from the
uninformed. Extracted from the boot where it had shed at
least three-quarters of its flowers, the plant then went
through an initiation ritual whereby it stood on the verandah
without water until it was minutes from expiring altogether.
Sometimes I got the timing wrong and the plant went straight
to the grave still wearing its label. The ones that got through
were planted in a hole hastily dug wherever there appeared
to be a gap. My reading had now raised the possibility of
an alternative to this somewhat *ad hoc* approach—the novel
idea of first considering the total effect and proceeding
according to a plan. It was simply a matter of deciding in
which direction to go.

The most controversial issue in the whole question of
garden design in this country is arguably that of native vs
exotic plants. Some years ago it seemed to have acquired the
dimensions of a moral crusade. As far as I could tell, the purist
view was embraced with greatest fervour by the more highly
educated in the community, reaching fever pitch in institu-
tions of tertiary studies. Apocryphal or not, an anecdote
involving a professor of botany at one of our universities

illustrates the emotional climate very well. This worthy academic was reputed to have cultivated with great care and patience three specimens of that beautiful extant fossil, the maidenhair tree (*Ginkgo biloba*). Years of loving care were rewarded when the slow-growing ginkgoes at last began to round out from their gawky juvenile growth into graceful trees. One fateful morning, the professor on his daily pilgrimage to the ginkgo corner found the trees lying uprooted on the ground, festooned with a placard bearing the warcry of the jihad: 'Plant Native'. I am not aware of whether this sort of botanic jingoism occurs in other countries. Certainly, British gardening writers seem to have a serenely eclectic attitude to all the flora of the world. Indeed, exotic plant collectors have traditionally been national heroes. What struck me as a curious feature of the debate in Australia was the fact that those who were most uncompromisingly purist in their insistence on native flora were also the loudest voices in the even more heated debate on immigration policy. The slightest imputation of discrimination against exotic homo sapiens and you'd need a whip and a chair to continue the conversation. Personally, I have nothing whatever against native Australian plants. I freely acknowledge that there are a great number of very beautiful species, particularly if one values subtlety over brilliant display. I must also say that I have now seen a number of exclusively native gardens which I admire very much. But I can see no compelling reason to believe that the inclusion of some foreign species in my garden is either a betrayal of my birthright or one of the more craven examples of cultural cringe. I must admit that I never really considered going native; possibly it was my experience with the grevilleas which set my feet firmly on the exotic path when I came to plan my new garden.

And exotic it certainly was. Again and again in my perusal of gardening books I found myself drawn to descriptions or depictions of the formal enclosed gardens of medieval times. My unfocused yearning was crystallized by a series of pictures of that grand re-creation of a monastery garden at The Cloisters in New York. This at once became my model. I'm not sure that the irony of copying a copy got through to me at the time. Pieces of paper covered in designs for cruciform parterres littered the house. Lists of medicinal herbs were compiled. Sundials were sought. Books on beekeeping were bought. The heavy arches which sit stolidly on our front verandah suddenly took on a distinct look of the cloister. Snatches of plainsong and matins were in the air. My husband, while largely impervious to the romantic aspects of the plan was persuaded that the proposed changes were a good idea on the grounds that they entailed levelling the front garden, the indecisive slope of which had always offended his sense of order. He gave his imprimatur and promptly left the country, a reflex action when upheaval looms.

It was at this point that I made one of those mistakes which are such a regular feature of this narrative. I did not consult a professional. Confident that I knew exactly what I wanted, I briefed a firm of builders who had worked on the house.

I knew them and liked them. Splendid builders and pavers they were; landscape gardeners they were not. My plan entailed raised beds around the fences (turf seats perhaps?) and a paved area to replace the lawn. This was to have a sundial in the centre surrounded by geometric beds arranged in a formal pattern. The area was duly levelled ready for the concrete pour. Did anyone think of drainage? Certainly not me. I was into design and aesthetics, not workability. There was much marking out of my patterns and with stakes and string on the rock-hard clay that stood stripped of any vestige of topsoil. I was the overseer of a group of bewildered Italians. One finally begged me to answer one question: 'Lady, what is it?'

After many delays due to rain (. . . why is it lying about in lakes like that?), the concrete was poured and inexorably set, precluding the possibility of ever doing anything adequate about the drainage. But for now the sun shone, no rain fell and the problem lay dormant.

We waited no longer than six months for the bricklayer's back to heal and his mother's funeral to conclude. When he saw the paving pattern I wanted him to follow, his disc shot out again and his father's hold on life started to look shaky. Under the lash of hunger, he was eventually coerced into finishing and a very good job he made of it. Changes in direction of the bricks have been used to suggest paths and an entrance, while the circular pattern round the sundial gives a central focus to the formal design. This sounds a lot grander in the description than the actuality, but I am happy with the result.

Renaissance in South Yarra

In the meantime, I was being ruthless with the existing vegetation. Here, advice from the Viscount Lambton had been invaluable in stiffening my wavering resolve. I had encountered his splendid words of wisdom in the course of reading (The Englishman's Garden) (Alvide Lees-Milne and Rosemary Verey), a book which has afforded me much entertainment and enlightenment. The Viscount is a man of decided tastes and unambiguous prose; 'Is there anything more hideous than an orange azalea?' is one of his more diplomatically couched observations. I quote further: '. . . it is I believe absolutely essential that dislikes should be held. Nothing is more irritating than a gardener who will say, "I dislike that tree but as it is a fine specimen I have left it there". Such tolerance is the destroyer of cohesion.' Guiltily aware of countless prevarications which would have driven the worthy nobleman into a state of terminal irritation, I resolved to mend my ways. The wheelbarrow became a tumbril as I set into all the orange and puce azaleas which I, in my feeble bourgeois fashion, had tolerated for years.

Out came the undistinguished camellias, the crooked alder and the antique apple tree. I must admit to some vacillating over the apple. It was a graceful old tree and I was very fond of it. I did go so far as to consult an expert who pronounced its remaining years to be very few. This sealed the tree's fate; I decreed its removal, telling myself it was euthanasia rather than aboricide. The tree ferns which were a sorry sight, reduced to one or two crisped fronds, also gave me pause for thought. Should they be returned to the wild where they unquestionably belonged? Lofty impulses like this never stay with me for very long, so I settled for moving the ferns to the shady side of the house with the others that had done well there. This was a success; the ferns recovered quickly and look infinitely better in groups anyway, which is the way they grow naturally.

On the whole, the clearing out was very therapeutic, like de-junking cupboards or cleaning out the shed. I have never missed any of the plants I pulled out. When we finished, the largely empty beds had all the promise of a blank canvas rather than a blasted heath. The Viscount was quite right.

In the good old days I would, at this point, have simply proceeded straight to the planting. But I had at long last begun to perceive a great truth; that the condition of the soil correlates quite closely with the welfare of the plants. I can't even claim to have deduced this truism of good husbandry for myself. It was an epigram in a forgotten magazine which had caused the light to dawn. I don't recall the exact wording but a rough approximation runs: 'Better a $1 plant in a $10 hole than vice versa'. This made a great impression at the time—indeed, it seemed to me to represent the apex of human understanding in the field, so I did go to some lengths to ensure that my rejuvenated garden was amply provided with $10 holes to accommodate the new plants in the style they preferred.

Advice on the best way of enriching the soil is freely available but a mite confusing. A bewildering array of substances is recommended for digging into the ground with a view to improving the structure. Given the fact that paper is among them, one could do worse than dig the $10 notes straight in and leave it at that. It would probably be as cheap a method as any. One of the newer and more fashionable nurseries in our city boasts a thriving and beautiful garden behind their shop. At this time it was less than three years old but had the appearance of having been established for decades. I asked what they had used to improve the soil before planting. It was a special chamomile compost I learned and, yes, it was available from the nursery for a trifling consideration. I bought one bag on lay-by and retired to consider the problem. The bag was labelled with a name and telephone number. I dialled it. They would be happy to supply me with compost at a wholesale price. How many truckloads did I have in mind? I thought I could get by with one truckload to start with, erroneously as it turned out. The stuff is pure magic. It is a crumbly dark brown, looks as if you could eat it and doesn't smell at all. I am now convinced it is all that is necessary to produce prodigious growth and dramatically improve soil structure. Three years ago I wasn't sure. I was spinning into over-kill mode familiar to all my near and dear ones and was worried that there might just be something missing. Surely compost should smell? I had a load of ripe cow manure delivered just to be on the safe side. It smelt; ergo, it was good. We also had to have a great deal of new soil to fill up the raised beds.

The labour force consisted of a smallish youth and me (not a giant). We toiled for days from sunrise till dark, filling beds, digging in goodness, digging out old roots, trying to make some impression on the mountains of soil and humus piled in the drive. Digging of the central beds I had to leave to the unfortunate boy. By this time they resembled clay pans and had to be prised open to insert organic material by brute force. I was working on filling the raised beds. It was difficult to get the levels right; from time to time my husband kindly pointed out bits I had missed as he passed by in his pinstripes on the way to the office. Eventually, with his assistance, all were evenly filled with what we hoped was a nutritious cocktail of all the things plants like best, and I was taken away in the wheelbarrow. Fortunately, my convalescence could be fruitfully spent with the mountain of catalogues I had sent for to plan the planting.

TUDOR
CONCEIT

*T*he most influential of the many books I read in the course of my planning were probably 'Classic Garden Design' by Rosemary Verey and a small history of gardening in Britain by Anne Scott-James called 'The Pleasure Garden'. As works of reference for me they were perfect; accurate and succinct with easily digested information accompanied by charming and helpful illustrations. This was where I would find lists of plants for my monastic garden. I was somewhat taken aback to learn from 'The Pleasure Garden' that leeks, radishes and beets were more likely to be found in the monks' walled enclosures than decorative plants. I wasn't ready for a potager in front of the house. The alternative seemed to be a garden devoted to herbs, with one bed for medicinal, one for culinary, one for dyeing herbs and so on. Even for me—not normally prey to such aesthetic scruples—this seemed a bit over the top in the suburbs of twentieth century Melbourne. Besides, the concluding sentence in the monastic chapter dampened my enthusiasm a little: ' . . . for the most part the monastery garden was subdued in colour, and the flowers small'. It all sounded rather dull and utilitarian to me, and I regretfully left the cloister and read on.

Elizabethan gardens, I learned, retained the square enclosed shape of the old monastic gardens but introduced all manner of frivolities just for the fun of it. Fancy knots, flowers, arbours, rose gardens, statues, striped poles, topiary and sundials were added to the traditional fruit trees, small fruits and herbs which were still cultivated as in medieval gardens. This was more like it. I shifted my sights a century or two and started making lists.

Fired with enthusiasm, I made a purist decision to confine myself to the planting of fruits, herbs and flowering plants of the Elizabethan period. Believing this to be a bold and innovative concept, I was a little downcast to later discover the existence of a sizeable Shakespeare Garden cult but, for now, I was an eager pioneer.

❧

The first decision to be taken was the choice of plant for the low clipped hedges which I envisaged outlining the shape of the geometric beds in the parterre (a term which sounded intimidatingly grand till I realized that it means 'on the ground'). I did consider box, would that I had gone no further. With a romantic notion of bees and nostalgic scent, I settled on lavender. No single decision has caused more anguish. Unless you live on a gravel hillside in Provence, I would urge you to consider using some less capricious plant than lavender for hedging; they are not hard to find.

Becuase of the diminutive scale of my beds (about 3m x 2m), I decided on a dwarf variety. An obliging wholesale nursery sold me two hundred dwarf blue lavenders. They were labelled *Lavandula angustifolia nana* but I thought dwarf blue was close enough. They had to wait in their pots for a month or so because of the bricklayer's back. Twenty percent died—not of neglect this time but apparently just for the hell of it. The nursery had no more, so I went

elsewhere. Did I want 'Munstead' or 'Hidcote' lavender?
What about *L. angustifolia rosea nana*? Well, it's not really
pink, sort of mauvish—quite close to blue actually. I have
never really sorted out this confusion which is not helped
by the fact that all these varieties are often incorrectly labelled
anyway. Trying to keep a lavender hedge in anything like a
uniform shape in heavy soil is a nightmare. How the
Elizabethans managed it on their soggy island I can't imagine.
A bush will die overnight out of sheer bloodymindedness.
If they decide to live, a whole row will suddenly come down
with a disease called shab which sounds and looks like a
particularly scrofulous skin complaint. Replacements have
been expensive and literally mixed—I now have a lavender
tapestry which includes *L. atropurpurea*, 'Munstead', 'Hidcote' and what could be a dash of French and Italian. Add
to all this the fact (recently gleaned from some authoritative
journal) that lavender has a very limited life span, and the
argument for hedging with box, rosemary or possibly small
wooden pickets looks very convincing. For all its drawbacks,
though, there is nothing so powerfully evocative of child-
hood, of grandmothers' gardens, of a sense of continuity of
gardening through the ages than this infuriating but endearing
plant. I wouldn't be without it; I just wouldn't try to use
it formally again.

❧

The same wholesale nursery supplied me with a decorator's
collection of herbs chosen solely on the grounds of appearance without the slightest consideration of their relevance

to the family menu. It was clear from the many books I consulted that the appellation 'herb' is an obligingly elastic one. It can be applied, it seems, not only to the remarkable variety of plants that have at some time been ingested in the hope of improving one's health or one's food, but also to any plant that someone once may have strapped on as a poultice. Optimism and experimentation were evidently salient features of the healing sciences in past ages; this definition embraces most of the genera on the planet. So when I came to choose my herbs, the range was considerably wider than I expected.

Silver leaves had a high priority. Curry plant (*Helichrysum angustifolium*), artemesia, rue, rosemary, grey and purple sage went into my shopping trolley first. There was also a sizeable group with names like heartsease, gilliflower, mugwort, feverfew and lambs' ears which had a nicely archaic ring. There was a collection of carpeting thymes for the sundial and bergamot, hyssop and lemon balm for the bees. Parsley, chives and basil which I used for cooking I continued to buy from the greengrocer. Too green.

I did order the herbs in multiples of three or more, but planted them singly, in a random muddle. They looked terrible, but I didn't know why. A more careful perusal of the text of a glossy American book on herbs ('Herbs' by Emelie Tolley and Chris Mead) yielded the excellent advice: 'Clustering several of one variety of plant together will have greater impact than growing single specimens.' Many times since I have encountered similar warnings against the perils of 'spottiness', a hazard to be avoided at all costs in all manner of plantings besides herbs. It is probably the single most important maxim of good design that I have acquired. All the herbs were dug up again and repositioned in groups. Much better.

❧

In planning the raised beds around the perimeter I persevered with the pleasant fallacy of a productive garden and began to choose fruit trees. An urgent need was for trees which would screen the houses opposite and foster the enclosed feeling I wanted. Still hankering after the vanished apple tree I ordered, at considerable expense, two mature fruiting apples to go on either side of a garden seat which had been set into a recess in the retaining wall facing the sundial. The trees duly arrived, their roots swathed in enormous hessian bandages. The delivery men unloaded them and left. We had lived for months with a bare front garden, so I regarded the trees in a state of some excitement. They were big and I was alone. One of my besetting sins is a strong tendency, in a fever of impatience to see results, to an impetuous approach to a task. A bad attack of this malaise struck now. I would plant the trees myself.

I dug an enormous hole and somehow hauled and levered a tree into position. Very gingerly, I unwrapped the hessian cocoon and the tree was lowered into the hole. Easy. The second hole was not so easy to dig—it was directly on the site of the old apple tree, and a fair percentage of its roots were still in the ground. Fatally, complacency had set in and I decided it didn't really matter; the new roots could simply make their way around the old ones I couldn't get out. I dragged the second tree up to the hole. This root ball was bigger than the first and in much stiffer clay. Tired and cranky, I tried to loosen it up, probably none too gently. Most of the huge clay ball broke off in my hands, along with the greater part of the root system. Going into my celebrated impression of a headless chook, I jammed the few vestigial roots into the inadequate hole and tied the tree to a vast number of stakes hastily pushed in to keep it upright. Two metres of tree supported by 30 centimetres of root.

Remorse ensured the most intensive care regime for the mutilated tree. Surgical pruning was performed at once. Daily doses of hormone and seaweed solution were administered. Hourly checks for hopeful signs and portents drew blanks. In early spring, the other tree burst into blossom and then vigorous growth. No change in the patient. Just as I had decided that I really had done for it, one or two of the buds began unmistakeably to swell. Relief and celebration as others followed and some blossoms opened. My ebullience was short-lived; from some dim recess of memory there came to me the fact, real or imagined, that plants whose survival is threatened will put their last burst of energy into producing seeds to ensure the continuation of the species. Was my tree going to live or were we witnessing a final floral convulsion? Had I confused trees with salmon? I unburdened myself of these worries to my husband when he incautiously remarked that the tree looked like surviving after all. He gave it a wide berth for a while, clearly reluctant to intrude on one of the darker mysteries of the Great Cycle.

The tree lived. This is even more remarkable than I had at first thought, given that it was planted amongst the roots of another apple tree. It seems that Specific Replant Disease—a mysterious ailment that affects some species of trees and shrubs if planted in soil that has previously grown the same species—affects apple trees particularly badly. (I am indebted to 'The Well-Tempered Garden' by Christopher Lloyd for this information.) Perhaps it was saved by all those hormones. It will take another year or two for it to catch up to the other tree which I plan to hobble every spring by a severe pruning, so eventually I hope to have a matched pair arching over the seat.

My other fruit trees had a less traumatic debut. A sturdy grapefruit and a small orange tree had survived the big clean-out. These regularly produce a crop but the fruit its so sour and crammed with seeds it is virtually inedible. Just as well; it looks much better on the tree. A small standard Meyer lemon was transplanted from the pot in which it had been confined for fifteen years. The relief was so great it produced an enormous crop of lemons almost at once. Two nectarines which I had bought already trained as fork-shaped espaliers were painstakingly tied into position against a sunny wall. In front of these went dwarf peaches, redcurrants and several small cumquats which I think are the most decorative of all citrus with their miniature pointed leaves and enamelled fruit.

To top up this cornucopia, I planted large numbers of strawberries as groundcover around the feet of the trees. While I like the look very much, they are not without their problems. The popular varieties sold by nurseries like 'Red

ALPINE- STRAWBERRIES

Gauntlet' and 'Royal Sovereign' succumb very easily, in my garden anyway, to virus disease regardless of how many guarantees accompany them. My first planting of what I thought were alpine strawberries could not be rated an unqualified success either. Instead of the real thing (*Fragaria vesca*) I put in dozens of a look-alike mock strawberry (*Duchesnia indica*). This is a very pretty plant with small yellow flowers and red fruit which has no taste whatever. Very invasive, it flings out runners with enthusiasm and leapfrogs at a great rate all over the garden. I am still trying to remove all of them and re-plant with real alpine strawberries which do not throw out runners, look beautiful for most of the year and taste ambrosial.

Under-planting the strawberries were a lavish number of white lilium bulbs. I did try the traditional madonna lilies (*Lilium candidum*) but with little success. I believe they tend to be temperamental, while *Lilium regale* has been much less fussy and looks most satisfactorily like the lilies clutched by every angel in Renaissance paintings.

Roses were to be the third major element in my planting scheme. Very shaky on all aspects of this superlative genus, I had nevertheless looked forward to making choices from a group I had categorized under the single heading, Old-fashioned Roses. I think my mental picture was after Rédoute; great glowing pink and striped peony-like blooms borne in abundance for long periods of time were what I had in mind. One simply selected the most delectable illustrations and sent off an order. Again I turned to books for help. My first reference, an excellent 'Dictionary of Roses' (Gault and Synge), quickly made it plain that my notion of old-fashioned roses was laughably simplistic. I was soon lost in a confusion of *Albas, Gallicas, Eglanterias* and *Damasks;* dazzled by luscious pictures of 'Fantin Latour', *Rosa mundi*, 'Felicite Parmentier', 'Great Maiden's Blush' or 'The Thigh of the Passionate Nymph'. I wanted them all. I became a compulsive buyer of books on roses, poring over the illustrations and even, on occasions, the text. Another of life's great disappointments awaited me between the covers; it was the dreaded addendum 'non-recurrent'. This was attached as a matter of course to any rose I found that was either historically 'in-period' or that I coveted for its sheer beauty. (Beauty in a rose I was by now judging according to its lack of resemblance to a hybrid tea. Now that's real sophistication for you.)

I found myself squarely on the horns of a dilemma that faces all owners of small gardens who hanker after old roses. Is it worth putting up with forty weeks of gaunt and prickly gaucherie for the brief glory of the flowering season? It was during the course of wrestling with this problem that the pure ideal of historical accuracy first became a little polluted. My reasoning ran roughly thus: the principal merit of the great majority of rose bushes is their flowers. As many others have observed, one would be unlikely to choose a rose as a foliage plant or for the graceful tracery of its bare branches in winter. Therefore, in a small garden, one must aim to have roses which flower for as much of the year as possible. Hardly a polemic to change the world, but painfully distilled from

many hours of reading and cross-referencing of rose catalogues. However, I didn't want the hybrid teas and floribun-
das which are so plainly products of the technological age
of hybridizing. There was only one thing to do—cheat. Back
to the books and catalogues in search of reproductions instead
of the genuine antiques.

The Bourbon roses seemed to fit the bill quite well. The
Elizabethans may never have known them, but they were
oldish, extraordinarily beautiful and were labelled in one
catalogue as perpetual flowerers. 'Souvenir de la Malmaison'
and 'Variagata di Bologna' went onto the order form. The
Chinas were clearly my sort of rose—they introduced the
recurrent gene in the first place. Half a dozen bushes of 'The
Fairy' went in among the herbs, along with several bushes
of the miniature moss rose 'Dresden Doll' which looks
positively medieval and was probably bred last week.

But the real jackpot came in the guise of a short article
in a horticultural journal on the English roses of David Austin.
They sounded too good to be true; gloriously pre-Raphaelite
in form, exquisitely coloured, scented as roses used to be
scented *and* miraculously recurrent in their flowering habits.
The few illustrations looked mouthwatering. Even the
Chaucerian names held charm for romantics; for those who,
like me, hanker after all things medieval, 'The Wife of Bath',
'The Reeve' and 'The Yeoman' were irresistible. Why had
this secret been kept from me? Mr Austin, I learned, had been
producing these paragons since 1969. Few nurseries in
Melbourne had even heard of them. Some determined
detective work led eventually to a trip to the country to meet

the author of the article, Mr Ross Boaden, who appeared to be the sole Australian grower. A most charming man, Mr Boaden showed me his collection of David Austin bushes, then in full flower. I was completely bowled over. Here was all the ravishing beauty of old rose paintings in row upon row of glowing colour. The agony was trying to make a choice. Fortunately, only a few were then available. I came away with them all: 'Lordly Oberon', 'Chaucer', 'The Reeve', 'Hero' and 'Cymbeline' were tenderly bedded down in the boot, and I drove home in a state of euphoria. Since then, David Austin roses have become somewhat better known and more readily available in Australia, but I am puzzled as to why they do not rank in popularity up there with 'Iceberg' or even the ubiquitous memory of Malmaison. I feel sure that one day they will. There is quite a range of sizes, from small bushes like 'Dame Prudence' to large shrubs like 'Hero', a recurrent Constance Spry look-alike which can be induced to climb to three metres. The best selection of photographs I have found to date is in Volume II of Trevor Griffiths' 'My World of Old Roses'. Once you have seen them, you will be hooked.

I had yet to resolve the question of what to plant in the two tiny square beds (holes, actually), at the 'entrance' to my formal garden. They had been put into the design purely to balance it, as the garden had to be centred on the house which does not sit in the middle of the block. They needed something simple and architectural. I considered an arch, standard roses or citrus, obelisks and topiary. None of them seemed quite right. Then I saw in a nursery some extremely narrow pointed conifers which were a good blue-grey colour, very similar to lavender. They were *Juniperus virginiana* 'Skyrocket'. Just the thing. They did look very smart planted in their little squares but the effect was marred by their bare ankles. So I bought sixteen more very small skyrockets and planted them as a hedge around the edges of the squares. They have been cut off at a height of about 30 centimetres and will eventually, I hope, form a clipped square base for the two larger trees which will be kept trimmed into smooth columns. Or that's the plan.

The sundial for the centre also presented some problems. Old sundial faces which work in the southern hemisphere are few and far between. New ones tend to be aggressively new, with very shiny faces. I bought one of these, which I didn't like, in the hope that it would quickly weather into indecipherability. However, it was built to withstand the worst of the elements in mint condition. Also, lacking a degree in quantum mechanics, we never have worked out how to set it so that it gives even a rough approximation of the time of day. I have recently discovered a firm in South Australia which makes beautiful sundials to order. One may specify the design and inscription. As soon as I can find or compose an inscription that is neither quaint nor morbid (all the ones I've seen have been either saccharine sentiments about sunny hours or dolorous warnings about fleeting or last hours), I will send off an order. I just hope it comes preset to tell the time.

Tudor Conceit *Bees*

In one corner of the raised beds we put a straw beehive on a low stand. It was surrounded by plants reputedly attractive to bees such as bergamot and hyssop. I do like very much the comfortably agrarian look of it, but the whole thing makes me uneasy. With a sinking certainty I know that I will very soon have to put some bees in it or stand convicted of a blatant sham. It seems to be taking an unconscionable time to read the book on beekeeping; I am not a born apiarist. Perhaps if I plant more bergamot the bees will take up residence without my assistance.

Some sort of screen had to be found for a tap which a plumber had installed, during the ten minutes I was out buying milk, in the most prominent position he could find in front of the house. Growing something in front wouldn't work as it was surrounded by paving. Perhaps some topiary in pots?

I love topiary; it is fun gardening. I pore over pictures of yew pyramids, box balls and hornbeam arches; my favourites are birds and animals like squirrels and doves and elephants. I would like to meet their owners; the decision to share one's life with a verdant pachyderm must indicate a fairly blithe spirit. But perhaps this would be shooting a little high to begin with. Some sound words of advice I'd once read, which recommended hedgehogs and sleeping turtles to novice topiarists, came to mind. The problem was that the wretched tap needed something with a bit of height to hide it.

At just the right moment, my sister gave me an elaborate wire peacock which was intended as a framework for creeping plants. This sounded both easier and quicker than sculpting shapes out of slow-growing box or cypress. Inspired, I ordered another peacock and two roosters. I like things in pairs; it seems a satisfyingly symmetrical arrangement. All the birds were firmly stood in large squat terracotta pots and needlepoint ivy planted at their feet. One of the roosters hides the tap very well. Topiary is a slow business though, even with ivy on a frame. My birds haven't got much further than hairy legs. I'm not sure how I'm going to keep their beaks or tail feathers sharply outlined when the time comes, but a certain blurring of detail seems to be acceptable. I can't make out every feature of those famous doves either.

At last, long after my husband had given up asking hopefully if I'd nearly finished, some sort of hiatus in the bedecking of the garden seemed to be approaching. The truth was that I'd run out of space. And money. Regretfully deciding against a striped pole or two or perhaps a mount, I settled back to wait for spring.

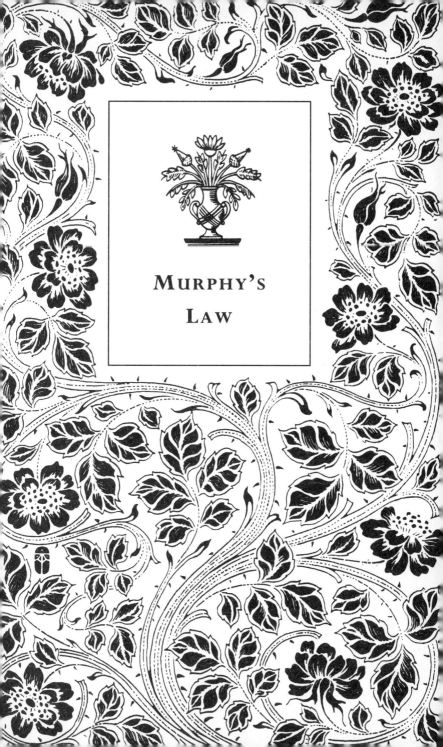

Murphy's
Law

*I*t was a very wet spring. Palliatives of the 'Well, it's good for the garden' variety were heard frequently. I was an adherent of this school of thought myself until one dark day when I stepped on the soil of one of the brick-edged herb beds in pursuit of a weed. My foot sank to the ankle. The entire bed was awash, a pool of mud confined only by the raised bricks around the edge.

The full implications of the situation sank in during the time it took to extract my shoe and repair to the house for a change of footwear. There was no way of getting drains into those beds without taking up the paving and concrete, a course of action my husband would have regarded, with some justification, as very adequate Grounds. It was one of those levelling moments in life; rarely had my bumbling amateurism been so evident. A more careful reconnaisance brought some comfort. The problem seemed largely confined to one bed. Digging into the soup as soon as the tide had receded a little, I found the dreaded clay a few centimetres below the surface. All the compost and manure lay on the top like decoration. The lavenders were dying off as I watched. Other natives of the Mediterranean didn't look too happy either. Drastic measures were called for. I gave myself furiously to think.

The first step was to dig out and repot all the plants in the bed, including the fifty lavenders; maybe they would revive. I then attacked the clay. Days of gouging and chipping and chiselling produced a hole about one metre deep and three-quarters of a metre across. Caked in mud and clay, I emerged from my burrow at night looking like a particularly bent and ancient garden gnome. When I could dig no more I declared the hole finished and filled it with gypsum, stones, coarse gravel and fine gravel, in that order. Little drains leading to this sump were excavated and filled with gravel. Then another trench was dug around the edges of the bed and all the clay removed and replaced with the sandy impoverished sort of mix which lavender appears to favour. All the top soil and compost were replaced and the bed was, I fervently hoped, ready for replanting. I had no idea if it would work but it was the only remedy that seemed feasible.

Because of the formality of the design, lavender had to be used again as a hedge in this bed, although it clearly hated the job. The thought of replacing the whole two hundred was just too depressing. I did try to salvage some of the old ones but it was a waste of time. Once lavender has decided that the time has come to shuffle off this mortal coil, there's nothing you or I can do about it. Eventually fifty new cuttings went into the still horribly damp soil.

The rest of the planting was chosen from hastily consulted lists of bog and swamp plants. I hoped with a sort of blind optimism that they might lap up some of the water that was drowning the lavender. White *Iris kaempferi*, white *Primula obconica*, opal basil and selection of mints which I found came in a wide and decorative range. Water mint (which sounded promising), apple mint, eau de cologne mint, peppermint and something called basil mint were all carefully planted in bottomless plastic pots in a bid to curb their enthusiasm.

The campaign for the swamp was not yet over. One more strategem suggested itself—worms. The clay must be broken down, I reasoned, and every weapon must be utilized. The situation plainly called for heavy artillery, so I ordered two thousand tiger worms from a mail order advertisement without having any clear idea of their mode of transport. I found out when a courier rushed in with a large box, conspicuously labelled 'Fragile' and 'Urgent', clutched to his smartly uniformed bosom. 'What is it?' he enquired as I signed the imposing document he proffered. The sight of his face when I told him I will remember warmly for some time.

It must be said that I did open the box rather tentatively. A pamphlet on worm husbandry was enclosed. As instructed, I excavated a hole in the bed and filled it with compost. Quickly upending the box over the hole and even more quickly heaping extra compost over the writhing mass, I retreated to a safe distance breathing rather fast. I do not normally seek intimate contact with invertebrates.

Just which of my extemporized drainage measures was effective I'm not sure but the bed in question, while not dry, is now much less sodden. Even the finicky lavender is, on the whole, consenting to live. A less welcome outcome was that the mints, wallowing in the moisture and loads of compost, roared away in all directions, effortlessly hurdling the paltry barrier of the rim of their pots, though I had left these protruding five centimetres or so above the surface of the soil. In six months they all had to be taken out again as they were strangling everything else. In the course of digging out the pots, I encountered a number of worms which looked like something out of Dune, so I assume that the conditions suited them. If they solved my drainage problem, I'm prepared to regard them almost with affection.

That first eagerly awaited spring brought a mixed bag of pleasures and problems. Pleasing combinations of colour and form began to emerge in some of the herb beds. Clumps of purple and grey sage merged with the fresh green of feverfew and lemon balm around a central bush of rosemary, the whole infiltrated by the peripatetic little viola known as heartsease or Johnny-jump-up. A bush of 'The Fairy' displayed its small pink roses through a froth of silver anthemis foliage and white daisy flowers. A small plant of *Nepeta* var. 'Blue Hills Giant' grew into an impressive bush covered in pale lavender spires. It flowered next to a sizeable clump of silver *Stachys lanata* and the David Austin rose 'Cymbeline', a pale pink beauty with faint greyish overtones. These small cameos were a source of delight and pride to the gardener who even inadvertently had arranged such happy blends.

But as the season progressed, there grew an uneasy suspicion that we were over-Iceberged. Let me say at once that I am an avid Iceberg fan. The flowers are charming in their freshness and simplicity and are unfailingly produced in great numbers for an incredibly long season. Even in a situation which is far from ideal, such as a stony slope or an east facing wall, I have found this great rose to be a faithful doer. But in the small space of my enclosed garden, the whole of one wall was occupied by the eight mature Icebergs which had escaped the axe and which had been planted in the days when a straight line was the only design premise of which I was aware. That year, galvanized by the unaccustomed fare of compost and manure, the Icebergs had excelled themselves. There they stood, each covered in hundreds of flowers, looking for all the world like a row of their namesakes. They were spoiling the balance; the other roses were not yet large enough to hold their own. A re-arrangement was necessary.

Our gardener moved one on his next visit. He worked very carefully; the bush quickly recovered and resumed full production. But he didn't have time in his brief spell to do any more. I couldn't wait for another two weeks, so I attacked the three marked for culling myself. It seemed a relatively simple matter to remove a few rose bushes, particularly as they were to be discarded. Unbeknownst to me, the whole procedure was fraught with hazard. I have made mention before of Specific Replant Disease, a phenomenon with which I am now intimately acquainted, but had never heard of as I rather perfunctorily dug out the roses, leaving any recalcitrant roots behind. I probably wouldn't have believed it if I'd been told. I still find it incredible that this amiable rose, like all of its kind, harbours a capacity for revenge which rivals Medea's. If one were ever tempted to anthropomorphize one's plants, this would be the time. The sheer malice with which the ousted favourite selectively poisons the soil to cause its successor to sicken unto death, to me suggests truly sentient behaviour.

Unaware of these subterranean machinations, I planted a 'Fruhlingsmorgen' rose in one of the spaces left by the departed Icebergs. Never has there been a more miserable mis-named Spring Morning. The rose produced a few stunted yellow leaves, then decided that the wick was simply not worth the candle. Mystified, I dug up the corpse for a post mortem. There were virtually no roots at all. Casting a few aspersions in the direction of the Teutonic constitution, I tried a 'Duchesse de Brabant' planted out of a container. Unimpressed with titles, the ghost of the Iceberg claimed another victim.

Baffled and cross, I turned to the experts. Not all books on roses mention Specific Replant Disease. I think they should. Replacing one rose with another is surely quite a common change that people want to make in their gardens. It can be disappointing and expensive unless two or three barrows of soil are removed from the site and replaced with fresh soil which has not previously grown roses. Having finally got this message, the next rose I tried, a David Austin 'Chaucer' looks like surviving, now that the necessary soil change has been accomplished. Those Icebergs have not yet gone, though. Small shoots have appeared around the site of each vanished bush. I treat them with the greatest respect. They may be after me.

Another careful plan that went awry was my colour scheme. It had been my firm intention to restrict my palette, apart from greens, to white, silver/grey and pale pink with a frieze of blue provided by the lavender. This premise was deeply flawed from the outset; most grey foliage plants have yellow flowers. Frequent use of the shears is effective but time-consuming. In a small garden it is a reasonable trade-off for some of the most silver of shrubs such as curry plant (*Helichrysum angustifolia*), wormwood (*Artemesia absinthium*) and cushion bush (*Calocephalus brownii*). I have since learned that a fairly severe cut-back in early spring will prevent flowering altogether but to begin with I hurried out to cut off each yellow flower as it opened.

The next defector from the grand plan was the lavender which proved to have flowers of a deep and vivid purple instead of the gentle azure I had in mind. It is quite extraordinary how many different hues can be adjudged by the writers of plant catalogues and labels to be 'pink' or 'blue'. 'Pink' can be anything from the shrillest salmon (watch for the descriptor 'coral') to a magenta which induces headache (a favourite euphemism is 'deep pink'). 'Blue' is almost never anything of the sort; the indigo-violet end of the colour spectrum is what they really mean. If you do get hold of a real blue like that of *Salvia azurea* it looks just awful with all the mauves and purples you will undoubtedly have already. On the whole, the clash between all the warring shades of pink was the hardest to sort out. Initially, I spent a lot of time pulling out salmon dianthus, puce rose campion (*Lychnis coronaria*) and carmine cranesbills. Even my thriving clump of Japanese Iris had to come out as they turned out to be mauve instead of white and were looking very sickly with the shell-pink 'Chaucer' roses behind them. In fact, I had a lot of trouble with the colour of all the irises I ordered. Some tall white bearded ones turned out to be most elaborately patterned with mauve stiches and frills and falls. Another clump of supposedly pale pink iris opened in a glorious show of purple and brown. It was not easy even to give this horror away, though I do try quite conscientiously to find good homes for any rejects. Irises must be peculiarly difficult to identify as to colour; the supplier has been highly reliable in all other purchases.

By dint of much clipping, moving and discarding, a reasonably coherent colour scheme emerged. An inverted Queen-of-Hearts mode set in; all banished plants were replaced with white flowered ones to avoid any potential clashes. There finally came a day when I laid down my shears and prepared to enjoy the painstakingly pastel picture I had laboured for. That was when the oranges and lemons began to ripen.

Preoccupied as I was with the vagaries of the flora in my charge, I paid scant attention to the activities of the local fauna. A bit of bait kept the snails away from the seedlings and the odd aphid was easily wiped off. This *laissez-faire* approach came to an abrupt end one day in late spring when, in the course of twenty-four hours, all the new shoots on roses and fruit trees were stripped to the bone by possums and a billion or so thrips turned every pristine flower on the Icebergs into a depressing brown mess.

Disbelief. Fury. Revenge. Gardener became implacable hunter armed with traps and sprayguns.

I vacillate uneasily on the question of pesticides. Certainly I am sympathetic to the viewpoint which argues against the indiscriminate spraying of 'good' and 'bad' insects alike. A praying mantis staggers around coughing piteously for an inordinate length of time if it is caught in the crossfire. Bees and ladybirds in their final throes can also call to mind The Princes in The Tower. The guilt is terrible. Resolutions are made, garlic spray is purchased. Then comes the morning after the most treasured plants have been decimated in the night by some voracious arthropod horde of biblical proportions. It's straight back to the hard stuff. Muttering rationalizations like 'It's an unfair fight; they (meaning the plants) can't run away', a sinister masked and gloved figure dispenses death in the afternoon from a pack on its evil back.

The greatest marauder of all, though, is protected from the final sanction. The possum in inner Melbourne must be the penultimate example of successful adaptation of a wild native species to an urban environment. It's better adapted than I am to life in this large city. Revelling in the hectares of parks and gardens and its status as a protected species, the possum population is in a phase of exponential growth. I am unsure of the diet of possums in the wild, but in the city nothing is more to their taste than the new shoots of shrubs and trees, the rarer and more expensive the better. Desperate gardeners set out traps at night which capture, not harm, the admittedly appealing creatures lured inside with pieces of fruit. There follows, in the early Melbourne morning, a scene worthy of a French farce.

Possum-bearing cars pass each other on bridges all over the city on their way to release their captives on the other side of the river.

I have been doing battle for years with our resident possum tribe. There is no question as to who has the upper hand: the possums are winning hands down. Nightly they carouse exuberantly around the roof, leaping from one level to another in frequent outbursts of *joie de vivre*. After a refreshing snack of new rose shoots, they repair to the trees to heckle the cat in the voices of irritable old men with catarrh.

Every folk remedy, every deterrent ranging from keep-off sprays to moth balls, have I used in a vain attempt to persuade the bandits that there is more attractive fare elsewhere. In accordance with one directive, vulnerable plants were surrounded by sticks soaked in creosote. These became handy perches to reach the succulent top shoots. Drawing pins were stuck upside down in putty along the fence top where the little brutes sat to devour the apple trees. They tap danced across these with contemptuous ease. We finally returned to the traps.

It was a tense morning when we caught our first possum. Resisting demands for instant liberation from my daughter and the suggestion that the trap be dropped in the swimming pool from my son, I gingerly placed in the car the wire cage containing an irate, urinating, defecating possum and headed off for an uncertain destination. Twelve kilometres minimum, said the man who made the traps, otherwise they beat you home. Feeling like a murderer with a body in the boot, I started looking for a suitable piece of parkland at the twelve kilometre mark. Every time I slowed down I encountered the suspicious gaze of a keen gardener hosing the lawn or trimming the edges. They *knew*. Hasty acceleration. Finding at last a deserted piece of bushland, I released the beast with maximum furtiveness and headed back over the state border for home. I have since discovered that several animal welfare organizations will take trapped possums. Presumably the animals are released in a humane fashion at a distant location. I really haven't enquired too closely; it's much less wearing on the nerves.

SHORT BACK
AND SIDES

*A*s the front garden began, albeit fitfully, to take shape it became increasingly evident that some work was needed on the other areas, particularly the back. I felt there was a certain lack of congruity in having an Elizabethan garden in the front and a grevillea sanctuary at the back. The back garden is an awkward shape. It is not very big, irregularly shaped and is much wider than it is long. Few brilliant design ideas sprang immediately to mind; for some time I stayed in the front garden and tried to ignore the back. It is, however, in constant view from the windows of the kitchen. There came a day when I was forced to confront the problem.

As more or less permanent features we had the old elm and the lemon-scented gums, a swimming pool, two espaliered plum trees, a shed, two patches of indifferent lawn, brick paving and high ivy-covered fences. And grevilleas. The first decision made itself. Fortified by a quick re-read of the Viscount Lambton, I hauled out grevilleas without mercy and consigned them to the tip. They were no good for the compost heap; they're far too intransigent ever to rot down.

The wooden shed behind the elm was ugly and conspicuous, stained as it was with an insistent reddish-brown timber stain, intended to blend in with natural surroundings but in fact doing just the opposite. So the shed and the old garden furniture were painted a very dark Brunswick green. Hardly original, but a very good colour in the garden. The sombre dark brown quarry tiles on the two small terraces were replaced with pale terracotta tiles. Already, things looked considerably better.

The chief difficulty with the back garden, apart from its shape, was that there was very little planting space. The ivy had long since taken over the beds around the perimeter. Flowering plants would have to be grown in containers or on the house itself. I have chosen to put some climbing plants on the house, supported by trellis which has been made to frame windows and doors, though this will present problems when we have to repaint. I'll worry about that when the time comes. Two climbing Icebergs are making a brave effort to flower in their usual profuse fashion round an east-facing window. On the whole, they succeed very well despite the limited amount of direct sunlight and the only problem is a tendency to mildew in wet weather. Another wall faces due south. I was tempted to plant 'Madame Alfred Carriere', having read often of this rose's tolerance of sunless situations, but decided instead to try espaliered sasanqua camellias. Madame Alfred's reported mature height of seven metres alarmed me somewhat—it's not a very big wall. The camellias (var. 'Cinnamon Cindy') have small, faintly scented pale pink flowers with deeper pink buds; the effect is very similar to that of apple blossom.

In one back corner of the garden some steps led down to the rubbish bins and an old gate. To screen this unlovely area, a double hollow brick wall, referred to by the builder as a flower box, was built to a height of about a metre. It ended in a wrought iron arch strategically placed to suggest a more romantic destination than the dust bins. The hollow wall was filled with soil and compost and planted with roses; a mixture of 'Clair Matin' and the ubiquitous 'Sea Foam', that indispensible element of every smart Melbourne garden. I was expecting great things of 'Sea Foam'. The few specimens that I had seen in bloom in nurseries looked healthy, vigorous and very pretty, with a noticeable variation from white to pale pink in the small, abundant flowers. Not only did I plant half-a-dozen bushes in the hollow wall but I bought an expensive two metre standard for a large pot which I envisaged as a focal point in the back garden, highlighted against the dark green ivy wall.

So far, reality has fallen a long way short of these rosy visions. The foliage is healthy enough, but the flowers have been disappointing to say the least. The buds seem to open already infested with thrips, which quickly turn the petals brown. After a heavy shower of rain, the flowers turn black. The few blooms which escape these twin hazards look, in my garden anyway, insignificant and anaemic. I have sprayed and watered meticulously. I have fed the bushes with every form of nutriment and nostrum known to rose growers; slow release pellets and fast release rose food, potash and liquid manure, seaweed and Phostrogen. My 'Sea Foams' are the vegetal equivalent of Strasbourg geese. The floral display remains infuriatingly sparse, discoloured and pallid. This is particularly frustrating in that (a) other people's 'Sea Foams' are a magnificent spectacle of massed pink and white, and (b) my 'Clair Matins', growing in identical conditions, are burgeoning and blooming profusely on their gratuitous rich diet and pampered treatment.

It seems I am not alone in my failure. I have encountered this curious antipathy between gardeners and particular roses on a number of occasions. A recent newspaper article in Melbourne contained a fierce invective against that charming miniature 'Nozomi'. This is a most reliable performer in my garden. I find it a useful and attractive ground cover, flowering generously and stoutly resisting pest and disease alike. The writer of the article could not find words to adequately express his contempt. 'Nozomi' was declared to be faint-hearted, lily-livered, spiritless. Any reader misguided enough to have planted it already was urged to lose no time in ridding himself of this wimpish weed.

Widely diverging views also appear to exist on the performance of 'Souvenir de la Malmaison' in the garden. I have several times read authoritative statements to the effect that this rose is difficult to grow and sparse in its flowering. I must say that this has tended to be my experience; I can't seem to get my Souvenir to flower freely. My sister, on the other hand, can't get hers to stop; if it is to be pruned at all, flowers and buds have to be cut off in the dead of winter.

It has been my distinct impression that this sort of capricious behaviour on the part of plants goes beyond that which can be ascribed to differences in growing conditions. Some sort of personality clash, a basic incompatibility between grower and growee, seems to be involved. Whatever mysterious forces are at work, I am forced to conclude that 'Sea Foam' and I are not meant for each other; its days in my garden are numbered.

Short Back and Sides

※

Most of the decorative plants in the back garden are grown in pots. I love pots; they are my favourite garden ornament. A thriving plant in a terracotta pot or a Versailles tub is a most pleasing sight. It speaks of interest and effort and expertise; here lives a gardener, and order reigns. I have been buying pots for half a lifetime and am firmly of the view that nobody, but nobody, makes pots like the Italians. The tragedy is that they insist on doing it in Italy, a particularly expensive distance from Australia. Local imitations, made from cement, haven't quite the right look and need lots of trailing plants round the edges to cast a kindly veil. A local potter did tell me recently, though, that large moulds for terracotta are at last being imported into this country from Italy, so hopefully it will soon be possible to buy the larger sizes here without incurring financial ruin.

After many years of buying, arranging and re-arranging pots (to the severe detriment of my back) I have distilled for my own use three rough rules of thumb concerning their placement in the garden. A single pot should be big; pots in anything approximating a row or line should be identical; informal groups of pots should be a judicious mixture of shapes and sizes but not colours. Like all my rules, I break them constantly but on the whole I find these guidelines pretty workable.

Container gardening is a peculiarly satisfying sort of gardening. There is a near total dependence of the plant on the gardener, who ministers directly to its needs without a lot of help from the good earth or the elements. Food is quickly exhausted in a pot and rain, except for the heaviest showers, doesn't seem to get in at all. Wind and sun dry out the soil with incredible speed. So the gardener must fuss about his potted plants like a good parent, feeding and watering and cossetting in what seems a more directly nurturing role than that of tillers of the soil who are, after all, just midwives to Mother Nature. Control is greater, so the glow of self-satisfaction is warmer when a plant thrives in a pot than when it does well in the ground.

The pros of container gardening are fairly obvious and have been enumerated many times elsewhere. At the risk of appearing an inveterate Cassandra, I thought it may be useful to run through some of the cons of the sport as I know it. Most of the problems I have encountered are related to water; either it doesn't get in or it doesn't get out. To take the last, and probably the worst, problem first I have been surprised and somewhat incredulous to hear more than one expert state that it is not necessary to crock the bottom of pots before filling with potting medium. I have lost so many mature potted plants because of bad drainage I find this difficult to believe. I am now fanatical about crocking; round here it has been raised to an art form. Layers of large broken pieces of terracotta, large stones, small stones, coarse sand and spagnum moss are laid down before soil or potting mix are even thought of. The mortality rate has dropped sharply since this routine began; I believe this to be more than just a happy coincidence.

Getting adequate water into pots is also not as easy as it

sounds. Terracotta pots in particular dry out at an amazing rate, especially in an Australian summer. On a hot day, I find they must be watered at least twice and more frequently for smaller pots in an exposed position. If there are a lot of pots, this can be a demanding routine. If one is away for a few hot days, the anxiety is awful. Minders never do the job adequately no matter what bribes, blandishments or threats are brought to bear. Once the soil in a pot really dries out, the particles unite in an iron-hard bond to resist the re-entry of moisture. The top looks wet, but the water somehow contrives to make its way out the drainage hole without wetting the bulk of the soil at all. Not surprisingly, the health of the pot's tenant suffers severely in this arid environment. A number of new products on the market offer some hope of relief. In particular, crystals which reportedly store 400 times their own weight in water for periods of up to a month show great promise. I have high hopes, though as yet it's a little early to tell.

Overfeeding is another trap for the well-meaning amateur. A container by its nature concentrates the fertilizer some-times to lethal proportions. Even if the plants survive the chemical barrage to which I have at times subjected them, they tend to drop every leaf in a highly visible protest. Trial and error have led me to the safety of pelleted slow-release fertilizers like Osmocote (I wish I had a mine of the stuff) and Maxicrop which, even if applied neat, seems to result in nothing more lethal than a strong smell of the pier.

Possibly as a gardener I am accident-prone (a thought which may have occurred to the reader before this), but I must mention an unexpected hazard I have met in pot gardening: wind. I am fond of standard plants in pots, the bigger the better. Several times after a high wind I have found one of my biggest standards lying on its side amid the wreckage of a smashed pot. The wind catches the head of the standard and overturns the whole thing—even the biggest, heaviest pots. We have had to have a number of strong brackets made which are fixed to the wall or fence at the level of the head of the standard. The plant is firmly tied to the bracket at the top. It works quite well as the foliage of the head conceals the bracket. Large plants which do not stand beside a wall are better, I have found, in wooden Versailles tubs; at least these are less likely to smash if blown over.

The question of what potting medium to use has also been a cause for concern. Advice from the experts varies. Over the years, a popular fiat from these luminaries has been to use something they are pleased to refer to as John Innes Potting Mix. I have never seen this for sale anywhere, despite repeated enquiry; nor have I ever found a garden supplier who will admit to having heard of it. In the absence of this magical elixir, which is evidently restricted to the most exalted initiates, I mix up my own brew of proprietary potting mix, soil, coarse sand, peat moss and Osmocote, resisting the urge to throw in a couple of eyes of newt and toes of frog. I don't believe that most prepared soil-less potting mixes contain enough nutriment by themselves, particularly for roses. Too much soil in the mix, though, will cause drainage problems. It's largely a matter of experimentation.

I have tried a vast array of plants in pots, with mixed results. The most successful have been citrus, bulbs, pelargoniums and, somewhat to my surprise, roses. The least successful has been *Ficus benjamina* or weeping fig which can frequently be observed shedding leaves and fretting to get back to the rain forest where it belongs. A standard weeping Lillypilly in a huge pot also looks, after ten years, as if it is suffering from bound feet. I don't know what the final outcome is when a big tree like that is confined indefinitely but given adequate food and water. Death or bonsai? I guess I'll eventually find out.

The back garden, then, remains largely green, though in the case of the lawn, this is using the term rather loosely. I cannot become passionate about lawn care; it bores me rigid. Turning on a sprinkler in the evenings is the extent of it, and I'm afraid it shows, rather, but we mow the heads off the weeds and pretend we don't notice. At least they're the right colour. The all-green background shows up the roses very well, and pots of annuals look quite important. I have learned at last that this is the only way old hands use annuals, and it is certainly easier and more effective than the dreaded bedding out.

From a gardener's point of view the most difficult parts of a conventional suburban plot are undoubtedly the long thin bits which run down the sides of the house. All too often they are gloomy wind tunnels which offer cold comfort to all but the hardiest of plants. Ours is no exception; one side in particular is in permanent shade, cut off from the sun by a tall house next door and the three golden ashes which are by now enormous and spread a thick canopy which effectively keeps out all the rain as well. I have combed through many books and articles on 'dry shade' gardening in quest of plants of iron constitution and stoical disposition. The conclusion I have reached after years of research and experimentation is that there is no such thing as a good dry shade garden. One may get some of the hardiest plants to survive in such conditions, but they always look as if they're enduring rather than enjoying life. We did install a drip hose system to see if wet shade gardening was any better. It was, marginally. Instead of looking starved and parched, the surviving plants merely looked starved. Some, like the palms and ferns, perked up considerably with adequate water; they don't seem to require much in the way of feeding, even with stiff competition from tree roots.

For other more demanding plants, some method of supplying nourishment which would not be immediately stolen by the tree roots had to be found. Foliar feeding seems to be the answer. Camellias and helleborus respond well to this when I remember to do it. Seaweed (Maxicrop) and Phostrogen solutions appear to be equally effective. Lamium (aluminium plant) and blue and white *Vinca minor* are doing quite well as ground covers; both are tough customers. So things were looking up; at least we had some reasonably healthy-looking greenery. The whole long stretch, though, looked formless and boring. Some structure was needed to pull it into shape.

Short Back and Sides

I bought twenty or so very small shrubs of English box (*Buxus sempervirens*). These were planted about a metre apart along the edge of the path, each one in a bottomless plastic pot sunk into the ground, the rim level with the soil. Close to the trees, the holes for the pots had to be chopped out of a solid mat of tree roots. The bottom of the holes was filled with a layer of stones and spagnum moss to discourage the robbing tree roots from growing in too rapidly. So far, the box is growing reasonably well. I suppose eventually the tree roots will grow up through the bottom and I will have to resort to foliar feeding but I hope the shrubs will by then be sufficiently established to survive. The plan is to clip them into a formal shape—I think balls— to give some much needed form to this awkward strip of garden.

The other side garden was even more awkward to deal with in that it is burdened with the re-located garage. I hate garages with such a passion that I have given considerable thought to the possibility of designing an attractive one. I have decided that this really cannot be done. I have never seen a beautiful garage. The best one can hope for is that it be inoffensive, inconspicuous or, best of all, invisible. One envies those fortunate few who have enough land to hide the garage away somewhere far out of sight, behind the hedges where the stables used to be, though the stables and their tenants were much less in need of concealment than their present day equivalents. When you think about it, there is no getting round the fact that a garage must enclose a large empty space and have a very large door, if indeed it has a door at all. How can this be made to look enticing? It can't be dressed up with pots—these are a distinct hazard at night. Covering the outside with creepers certainly improves things, but there is still that yawning space inside or the large blank door.

I have seen some brave attempts to bring some glamour to this most mundane of structures. Trellis in various guises is currently popular in Melbourne, but a garage made of trellis can look like a strangely empty summerhouse. My favourite piece of ambitious garage design is in a seaside suburb of Melbourne and is evidently the *chef d'oeuvre* of a motorist with a classical bent and sturdy chequebook. The side wall of the garden is lined with niches from which life-sized Greek and Roman deities bemusedly contemplate the car's progress as it sweeps down the drive and into a passable facsimile of the Temple of Athena Polias. A courageous approach to the housing of twentieth century chariots, but perhaps not suited to every site.

Our garage is the doorless or carport variety. Originally the drive and garage floor were covered with concrete but this has recently been replaced with brick pavers which is a great improvement. I decided it would make things worse to try to tart up this area with flowering creepers or roses. Better perhaps to frankly admit that here we have a garage and leave it at that. A row of narrow Skyrocket junipers (*Juniperus virginiana*) has been planted right down the side fence and an army of ivy cuttings is gathering strength for the task of covering everything else in sight. I do have a little group of three box balls of varying sizes to add a bit of interest, but they haven't been in long and are currently rather underwhelming. I find box and junipers require the patience of Job, a worthy with whom I have little in common.

BUT IS

IT ART?

*H*aving looked over the previous chapter it occurs to me that someone who has just described in considerable detail her efforts to create a Tudor garden in the suburbs of Melbourne is on very shaky ground in being ever so slightly superior about someone else's version of a classical garage. This has led to some reflection on the vexed question of style, which I touch on somewhat diffidently, uneasily aware of total lack of qualification to do so.

I believe that most amateur gardeners have, to begin with, no idea of style at all. I am here assuming that the term 'style' is used in the sense of having an overall vision of what the garden will look like and working, however loosely, within this preconceived plan. Most of us begin by buying individual plants because they appeal to us for some reason—usually their appearance when in full bloom. Beginners plant them wherever there is a space; those a bit further down the track to becoming a gardener will choose a position that suits the plant. The next step is to consider further whether the new plant will look well with its immediate neighbours and so on. It is gardening by accumulation and the results can be serendipitous or disastrous. Many gardeners never progress beyond this phase and simply go on buying and planting and pottering and generally having a good time. Others move on to complicate their lives by fretting about axes and vistas, bones and spottiness, formal or cottage, native or exotic. Whether or not this shift to a more sophisticated way of thinking about gardening is made in a solo fashion via books, or with the help of a professional garden designer, the worrying issue of style vs fashion will sooner or later rear its head. Some landscape designers are at the cutting edge of the latest trend; some merely follow it. Others are true originals who create individual gardens to suit client and site. It has emerged from my reading that the doyen of this last group is the English designer Russell Page. Unfortunately I found his austerely intellectual and authoritative book 'The Education of a Gardener' rather late in my career. I almost wish I hadn't found it at all. In certain passages I could feel his stern eye directed right at me:

> I would like to differentiate between real style and the eclectic use of a style borrowed from another period or another place. This will be a reflected mannerism deliberately imposed . . . Any time or in any place contemporary styles and techniques are sure to make a pastiche of a style borrowed from another period. Such borrowings are fashions rather than styles and like all fashions sooner or later become dated and unfashionable.

Mr Page is undoubtedly right. It is a simple matter to compile a list of convincing arguments against the plagiarising of a style of gardening from another time or place. Leaving aside for the moment the tricky question of artistic integrity, the two which spring most readily to mind are, firstly, the possibility of a mis-match between the borrowed style of garden and the architecture of the house it surrounds and, secondly, the impracticality of the plants involved in the scheme.

But is it Art?

The current craze for cottage gardening which has swept through Melbourne like a bushfire is a case in point. A complicating factor is that the term is here used very loosely; it has become confused with another very English concept of the herbaceous border. For most, cottage gardening means purchasing a variety of 'old-fashioned perennials', taking them home and planting them either in a random fashion behind the newly installed picket fence or in more orderly beds surrounding the lawn. I do not intend to be in the least disparaging in my observations; I have done very much the same thing myself. In many cases, the end result is very successful. Older, smaller houses in this country are well suited to the 'cottage' style of gardening in that many of the features of domestic architecture in the last century were also borrowed from the home of the cottage garden. Small Victorian houses in particular look wonderful in the middle of the 'deliberate sweet disorder' currently so highly prized. It suits the style of house much better than the mahogany gums it probably replaced. Where the trend runs into trouble is when it tangles with more modern styles of house like the California bungalow, or larger and more imposing buildings. As I write, a relatively new block of flats in the next street is sporting a row of foxgloves right along the front fence. They look about as appropriate as a hitching rail for horses.

Ths cottage style of garden, then, does not transplant universally well. The same could be said for the plants themselves. Around these parts in recent years there has been a rush to rip out the old and put in the new (that probably should read the other way round). Delphiniums and foxgloves are everywhere springing up where cassias and banksias once held sway, grannies' bonnets are usurping kangaroo paws, paeonies replacing the hardy petunia. My garden was as ruthlessly Jekyllized as any, my planting lists apparently compiled for a vicarage garden in Gloucestershire. Doubts about the total wisdom of this course began to creep in as spring passed and summer got under way. Foxgloves drooped in 40 degree heat, delphiniums were smashed and scattered in the first roaring northerly, campanulas flattened by torrential spring rains. The leaves of *Alchemilla mollis*, instead of collecting glistening raindrops in the prescribed manner, scorched to a crisp in the summer sun. Paeonies, on the other hand, failed to produce a single flower because the winter wasn't cold enough. Things were not going absolutely according to plan.

I can now see, with the benefit of hindsight, that my whole gardening career has been a succession of shifts and changes made in response to current trends in design and planting. This insight is not a particularly welcome one. I, like everyone else, cherish an image of myself as a gritty individualist untouched by passing popular fads. I can say with a fair degree of honesty that I do not consciously follow a trend; shifts in taste and changes in ideals of beauty are brought about by a subtle conditioning process to which everyone is subject to a greater or lesser degree. There was a time when no room was ever photographed for a glossy magazine without a flourishing Kentia palm somewhere in evidence. The plants eventually acquire, by virtue of repeated association with beautifully decorated rooms in prestigious pubications, an aura of beauty in the eye of many a beholder, myself included. It doesn't matter whether one is a reader of these publications or not; the images slip into some level of awareness from covers glimpsed in bookshops, from newspapers, from films. There is no escape. One yearns for, covets, lusts after Kentia palms. They are solicited from indulgent relations at Christmas. Somehow or other, they are acquired. At precisely this point, they who decide what we like will decree that the palm hitherto used in all their shots be changed to a weeping fig. The imprinting process begins again; not a conscious process at all, just a dawning realization that it is time for a change in the house plants towards a lusher, leafier look. Why didn't I think of it before?

This sort of unwitting trendiness is, I believe, essentially an amateur response. The distinguishing feature of a true professional seems to me to be the ability to operate independent of fads and fashions in gardening or indeed in any other field of artistic endeavour. Professionals have the enormous advantage of knowing their field. At the very least, they must be aware from the outset that a trend is a trend and not an inspiration in the 'Eureka!' class, as I fondly imagined my Elizabethan plan to be. This is a good reason, I think, to consult an experienced garden designer if you are contemplating a sizeable investment in permanent garden features like paving. It would be very useful to know that the design you had set your heart on was soon to be, or worse, had already been, installed in every third garden south of the twenty-eighth parallel. If you happen to hit on a consultant who is an original, he or she will almost certainly come up with something much better anyway. You may even get some drains into the bargain.

But to return to the amateur. As well as being herded down the road to a particular style of garden by those savants who decide what will be photographed and written about, our errant fancy is guided by another, more personal factor. People are attracted, I believe, to a certain style of garden because of basic personality type. Those fortunate mortals who have a relaxed, *laissez-faire* attitude to life in general will be inclined to develop a garden along the same lines. They will favour natural landscapes, bush gardens, wild gardens. They will read with pleasure about meadow gardens without wondering how on earth the owners put up with all that unmown grass. They will not fuss about weeds or neat edges; nor will they begrudge the odd insect a bite or two on the way through. They own dogs. They are able to sit at their leisure and actually enjoy looking at their gardens without leaping up to deadhead a rose or spray an aphid. They are indeed a race to be envied.

At the other end of the personality scale are the gardeners to whom control is of paramount importance. The chaos out there must be kept at bay with high walls, clipped hedges, rows of matching trees, paths that know their own mind and don't wander about indecisively. This type of personality, which would probably be labelled by the Freudian school as anal-retentive, is comforted by a symmetrical arrangement of beds (preferably uniformly edged), by regularly mown lawn, plants safely contained in pots, espaliered trees, groves which nod at groves. Topiary is popular as a decorative art. A high percentage of this group would cite Villandry and Vaux-le-Vicomte as ideal gardens. The garden of the Viscount Lambton (who will be paranoid as well if quoted much more often) would also be much admired, particularly the rows of square trees. Gardeners of this ilk will put seats in their gardens because that's what you do, but they will *never* sit in them. There is always one more thing that is not right. Let me tell you it can be very tiring at times.

Is the amateur gardener, then, doomed to struggle on forever without real style, whipped along from fashion to fashion by 'Vogue Living' and his or her own relentless psyche? Striving to produce their vision of paradise only to have it condemned by experts as a 'sentimental and unedu-cated idea as to what a garden should be'? Probably. Some amateurs, of course, become so involved in their hobby and so expert through a process of self-education, that they move into a different league. Some few of these have great talent as well, their achievements surpassing in beauty and orig-inality those of many professionals. Vita Sackville-West was obviously one such. But I suspect most of us will continue to drift with the current of popular taste, changing our style of garden and collection of plants accordingly.

The immediate reaction of those accused of such sheep-like behaviour is to hang the head in guilty acknowledgement and fall to inscribing circles in the dirt with the toe. Before, however, we shuffle shamefacedly out of the garden alto-gether and take up indoor bowls, it may be worth considering for a moment whether our crime is after all so heinous. Mr Russell Page, whose stern judgement is quoted above, is demonstrably a giant, a genius among landscape designers. He has created gardens all over the world which will unquestionably endure and be admired for generations. He has also, surprisingly, never owned a garden. More particularly for the sake of this discussion, he has never owned a small garden. Large gardens can supply abundant variety and change within their own boundaries. It must be pleasant indeed to enjoy the meadow garden in spring when flowering bulbs bejewel the grass, to visit the summer border at its height, to sit and admire autumn in the water garden. Roll on the day when I can do it.

But the average suburban garden can be seen in its entirety almost at a glance. The yearning for change can be satisfied only to a limited degree by the seasons or a switch from white petunias to blue. How much more exciting to have a complete renovation; to sweep away the Victorian fernery or the Japanese contemplation garden that never quite worked or the patch of urban bushland and start again with a rose walk, a cactus garden, a formal vegetable potager or a parterre. Or a little of each.

It is possible of course to make changes in garden style and planting without being in the least trendy. I'm sure some individuals do, just as others are perfectly content to fix on or evolve a style and stick with it without ever feeling the urge for a new look. But I believe these are rare beasts. A much more common species, seduced by the ever-increasing number of luscious gardening publications, many from the northern hemisphere, finds itself quite suddenly possessed of the conviction that nothing could be more desirable than old roses with lavender or that the sooner white and silver assume their rightful place as the sole components of the horticultural spectrum, the better.

As a long-term member of this school, I feel I can say without giving offence that it is difficult to defend this behaviour on any grounds at all. It is mindless, it is expensive, it lacks any trace of creativity or integrity. It is also quite good fun. Resisting the whole conditioning process referred to earlier is an active and exhausting business, requiring a good deal of will, time and thought. Or sheer perversity. In an attack on garden trendies which appeared recently in a local newspaper, the writer appeared to advocate, as a desirable alternative, the use of bonfire salvia and African marigolds. Together.

Hurrying on, I have no doubt that the hammering out of a uniquely personal code of taste is a worthwhile endeavour and time well spent. It's just that few amateurs, by definition, can find it. Easier surely to potter about at the weekend planting white and silver plants, generally enjoying oneself and doing very little harm. I'm all for leaving the yucca and red-hot poker combinations to the rugged individualists. I'm sure they'll be very well suited.

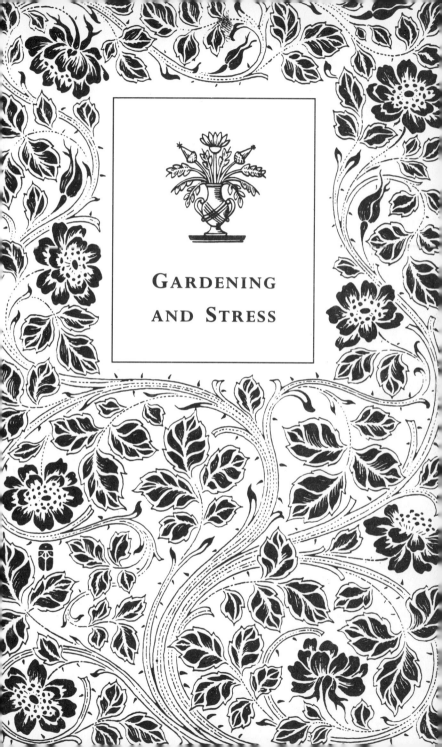

GARDENING
AND STRESS

*I*t is important to state firmly at the outset that gardening can be very stressful. Or it can live up to its popular image as an endless source of relaxation, reliably transforming its devotees from overwrought 'Type A' personalities to serenely tranquil 'Type B' individuals by the end of the first row of runner beans. As with any other form of human activity, it all depends on how you go about it.

I offer the following observations on the subject firstly as a gardener who is well acquainted with the pain as well as the pleasure of the craft and secondly as a psychologist, which is how I occupy my time otherwise. It may be of some interest, and perhaps benefit, to identify a number of the major sources of stress in gardening and to outline some pragmatic solutions I have arrived at together with a bit of theorizing thrown in.

*F*AILURE

A rich source of anxiety and depression in all human endeavours, failure in the garden comes in a number of guises. The simplest yardstick of success is the health of the plants in your domain. Possibly the most conspicuous instance of horticultural failure is when a plant actually dies. In certain circumstances—if, for example, the plant in question is an orange canna presented at Christmas by Great-aunt Maude— this may be a cause for relief, if not celebration. For the most part, though, the death of a plant, particularly a favourite, is distressing and fraught with guilt.

Another source of frustration, while not as traumatic, is the failure of individual plants to thrive. The sight of weak or stunted growth, yellowing foliage, sparse or absent flowering, general lack of health and vigour is almost as great an irritant as a corpse.

Whether the problem plant is dead or merely struggling, there is usually only one effective course of action—remove it with all possible speed. It's in the wrong spot. (Unless of course you've dropped a bucket or planted a boot squarely on it). It has been my experience that first-aid measures such as increased feeding or watering are strictly temporary in their effects and are decidedly not worth the effort involved. On the contrary, when these ministrations slacken off, as they inevitably will, the demise of the ailing plant is probably assured. Much better to adopt a firmly Darwinian stance and cull mercilessly. It is of course worth trying the patient in a new positon if it is not yet moribund. A wetter/sunnier/ shadier position frequently has a marvellously tonic effect on a sulking plant. If, however, there is no suitable or vacant space, remove the source of frustration anyway and throw, or give, it away. The relief is palpable.

The obvious preventative measure for this form of gardening stress is to inform yourself before the event of the growing requirements of the things you intend to plant. It is a relatively simple exercise, too. Leaving aside the vast numbers of books on the subject, a surprising amount of information of this nature is printed on the labels of plants in garden centres. 'Full sun' it says in black and white. 'Well-drained soil'; 'sheltered position'. So you've been told. A somewhat more difficult step is accepting this information. I have in the past leant heavily towards the 'triumph of faith over experience' school of thought in my placement of plants. It is a beguiling philosophy. Its major flaw is that it doesn't work. After many ill-fated attempts to grow roses without sun, or hellebores in it, or hostas in dry shade, or lavender in clay, it is my firm opinion that the writers of those labels are on to something and their instructions should be followed to the letter. To fly in the face of such collective wisdom is to virtually ensure disappointment. I try harder now to comply with these recommendations for the things I plant, but if they still refuse to perform, they go. Thinking of it in this way also rather neatly shifts the blame, I find.

Disappointment, being the reverse side of the coin of vaulting ambition, is a fairly constant companion of the keen gardener. Rarely do the results of one's labours measure up to the gorgeous visions conjured up in the excited imagination by picture books and coloured catalogues. An excellent anodyne for the deep sense of inadequacy generated by these pictures of impossible perfection is to remind yourself frequently that this was the only ten minutes of the year that the said plant/garden looked 'just so'. A week after the photographer departed it probably resembled much more closely the scene outside your own windows.

While individual plants can be aggravating enough when they fail to live up to expectations, the potential for despair is greater when carefully conceived design schemes go awry. Pictures painstakingly composed in the mind's eye and planted out with care and high hopes fail to materialize or are swiftly obliterated because of the overbearing nature of one or more of the elements. With uncounted disasters of this nature under my belt I feel I can offer, with a certain degree of authority, two cardinal rules which should be embraced as a personal code by the aspiring designer:

1. Ascertain the mature height and spread of any plant under consideration for inclusion in a scheme.
2. Believe it.

As before, the first step is easier than the second. Transgressing these rules has been the biggest single cause of failure in my garden. And here I must lay some small blame at the august feet of that high priestess of the art, Vita Sackville-West. To a greedy gardener such as I, her advice to 'cram, cram, cram every chink and cranny' was licence to do just that, to a degree she surely never envisaged. Possibly it was not Miss Sackville-West's intention to encourage the planting of the entire contents of Sissinghurst in a quarter-acre patch—I'm not sure she'd ever seen one. Nevertheless, when her message reached inner suburban Melbourne, that was roughly the result, and the years since the first plantings have seen a more or less continuous process of removing, relocating, cutting back and wondering what on earth happened to all the things that disappeared without trace in the battle for survival.

In the interest of future peace of mind, it is a sterling idea to find a mature specimen of any more or less permanent plant you may be considering and to take a good, long look at it. Because yes, they really do get that big.

Gardening and Stress

GARDEN MAINTENANCE

In discussing this potentially burdensome aspect of gardening, I have assumed that the reader is a keen but amateur gardener, with limited time and a minimum of professional help. For this species, common in Australia, a garden which is not adequately maintained will be a nagging and even significant source of stress. For those who care about gardens, the sight of roses that need dead-heading, perennials that need staking, trees that need pruning, lawns that need cutting, weeds that need pulling and herbs that have run to seed will act as a constant irritant, cancelling out most of the pleasure to be had from the plants that look as they should.

The chief enemy, of course, is time. We are not averse to fixing all these problems—indeed, would actively enjoy it—but when, oh when, can it all be fitted in? I believe that the answer lies in part, at least, in developing a few simple time management strategies to ensure that (a) the jobs get done and (b) time spent in the garden is a source of pleasure and relaxation rather than a frenetic race against the clock.

Before elaborating on this point, though, one or two remarks on the question of style may be helpful in this context.

Stress and Style

Two fairly common traits discernible in the keen amateur gardener are ambition and optimism, attractive qualities both, but sometimes responsible for decidedly impractical decisions. Pedestrian though it undoubtedly is, it must be said that much angst can be avoided by making a realistic choice of style in the first place. A formal garden, to take an extreme example, can be very stressful for the amateur. This is gardening at its most labour-intensive. The box hedges and the mop-head standards need a haircut more frequently than the children. Without constant attention, the knot garden quickly becomes a mad woman's knitting. The inevitable casualties become major calamities. How to find a replacement of the right size for the pencil cypress that died right in the middle of the row? A football leaves a gap like a missing tooth in one of the espaliered fruit trees. This is the stuff of serious neurosis. A more informal arrangement where a little asymmetry or unruliness is acceptable or, better still, desirable is far less wearing on the nerves. Little wonder that the cottage style has proved so durable.

Professional Help

This is becoming a luxury both in the house and in the garden. However, if it can be managed, an hour or so a week of professional tidying up in the garden is a valuable investment in stress reduction. It is an inescapable fact that whatever style of garden is involved, unless lawns are cut and paths swept regularly; it cannot look anything but unkempt and therefore depressing. Performing these chores yourself has three disadvantages. Firstly, they are boring and time-consuming jobs which keep you from more enjoyable gardening. Secondly, they must be done all over again with disheartening regularity. And thirdly, you won't do them. If it's at all possible, it is much more rewarding to spend your time in the more creative areas like planning and planting or even doing long-term maintenance jobs like pruning and mulching. At least these don't have to be done again next week.

In this context, it is worth noting that propagation is one of the most rewarding of all gardening activities. There is great satisfaction to be had from growing from seed, getting cuttings to strike, or simply producing five new clumps of a perennial from one ageing one. Even more satisfying is the virtuous awareness of the great economies being effected by all this multiplication, assuaging a conscience uneasy about the alarming cost of that last load of compost or the new bird-bath. I was inspired to learn from the gardener who created the very large and beautiful herbaceous border in the Botanical Gardens that her grant to establish the entire border was $200. This was to include the purchase of manures, compost, fertilizers etc., as well as plants for a huge area. Her diverse and prolific collection of perennials has been built up largely from seed, division, barter and gifts. These ways and means of stocking a garden are readily available to all; gardeners are the most generous of species. And you can always liberate a cutting or two from an especially desirable plant that is hanging untidily over a fence. After all, the plant will benefit from the pruning. Though just to be on the safe side it's probably better to make sure that no-one is watching.

Avoiding Physical Stress

It is stating the obvious to point out that it's difficult to enjoy oneself and be physically uncomfortable at the same time.

Being too hot/too cold/too tired distracts and detracts from the pleasure to be had from any form of recreation. Yet gardening is an activity that all too frequently involves all of these states. It is often strenuous and, for the serious practitioner, is carried on in all manner of weather and site conditions. Some attention to details of dress, equipment and work habits is useful in minimizing physical stress. If one is dressed appropriately, it is possible in this country to be quite comfortable working in the garden in any season with the possible exception of high summer. For much of spring and autumn, of course, it is a pleasure to be outside gardening in any old clothes that come to hand. Useful aids I have found are:

1. Gardening shoes that are in fact plastic clogs from Germany with liftout washable insoles. These can be taken off at the door without using hands (very important) and are not fazed by being constantly hosed down or buried in dirt, unlike countless durable numbers I have ruined before I found these clogs at a local nursery.
2. Rubber gloves—the household variety. They don't last long, but they're cheap. I have never found a pair of gardening gloves that actually work—there is as much dirt inside as out, and cleaning them is a physical impossibility.
3. A straw hat chosen for propensity to stay on rather than decorative effect.

In winter, this fetching ensemble is augmented with another layer or two and a shapeless jacket of great antiquity that will soon have to be consigned to the compost bin, the contents of which it already closely resembles. To replace it I am hoping to secure one of those quilted sludge-green sleeveless jobs that appear to be some form of national dress in the Mother Country. I must say they do look just the thing for a spot of digging on a chilly day.

Having arrayed yourself in whatever outfit you deem suitable to the day, spend a minute or two arming yourself with a few props and aids to the good life. Some suggestions:

1. A pair of sharp secateurs. Easily the most gratifying implement in the gardener's armoury. Half an hour of vigorous cutting and trimming unfailingly produces that warm glow of achievement which is such a vital factor in creating an 'up' mood.

2. A large stout plastic bag for the 'Yard Mate'. This gadget is an indispensible wire stand which holds the bag in an upright position ready to receive all prunings etc. It saves an enormous amount of fumbling about when cleaning up. The filled bags are easily tied up and stacked in an obscure corner while the contents turn themselves into quite passable compost.

3. A radio or, better still, a Walkman. It doesn't matter if your preferred entertainment is a football match or Bach fugues; having it there enhances the feeling that this is, after all, recreation.

4. A portable telephone. A real indulgence, this could be classed as a very optional extra. It is, however, bliss not to have to sprint through the house trailing blood and bone towards a telephone which always stops ringing as you reach for it.

This list could be added to indefinitely—a Thermos, jelly beans—the important thing is that you are going out there to enjoy yourself, so approach it in this spirit.

When, fortified by all manner of creature comforts, you actually get round to starting work, the trick is to stay comfortable. Depending on your work habits, you will work either in a state of relaxation or of stress. Shed or add layers of clothing according to the temperature. Sit whenever you can; stooping for any length of time is exhausting. A small stool is an excellent gardening tool, much more comfortable, I find, than those kneeling contraptions. Weeding, for instance, can be most satisfying therapy if you are at your ease while doing it. Whatever you're doing, it is imperative to monitor yourself frequently for muscular tension, particularly in the shoulders and neck. If you have built up a rigid set of muscles in wrestling with some especially recalcitrant onion grass, stop. Take a few deep breaths, drop your shoulders and relax your neck. It may be helpful to have a mental picture of undoing the muscles in the neck one by one until the head feels free, balancing or floating on top of the spinal column like a balloon on the end of a string— a method central to the Alexander technique and an effective relaxation procedure. It is astonishing how often this checking must be done to start with—the tension can return to the neck and shoulders in seconds if the habit is entrenched. For many people, relaxing in the garden—or indeed anywhere else—takes a great deal of practice. There may be some who feel somewhat self-conscious walking about pretending to be a balloon. Don't worry about it. The great thing about a garden is that it's very hard to startle the inmates.

Time Management

This really is at the heart of the matter. Stress (the bad sort) occurs when coping resources cannot keep pace with demands. In many instances, time is the key factor in this equation. The problem of insufficient time is exacerbated in gardening by the very characteristic which makes it such a stimulating and dynamic interest—constant growth. Even in the lowest maintenance garden there are chores to be done at all times and every day that passes adds to their magnitude. This can become a real problem for the type of gardener profiled earlier—the busy amateur with limited time who cares about her garden. Because she cares, the sight of plants in need of attention will be stressful and, in time, depressing. One of the symptoms of depression is inertia. So, in the little time that is available for gardening, she will be increasingly inclined to do nothing, mouthing rationalizations about not knowing where to start. Doing nothing will quite quickly result in a burgeoning wilderness, which leads to further depression, and so on.

In the context of gardening, the cycle of depression could not be said to operate on a grand scale, except perhaps in the most obsessive personality. For most, it is unlikely to lead to suicidal moods or black melancholia. Nonetheless, the feeling of being overwhelmed is quite sufficient to prevent one from deriving much pleasure from the garden, which is a pity, and any work undertaken is done in a half-hearted or despairing 'I'll never get done' fashion which is anything but pleasurable or relaxing.

One of the most effective weapons against depression and inertia is structure. Almost any sort of structure—a set of instructions, a list, a timetable, a plan—immediately begins to reduce to manageable proportions the chaos which threatens to overwhelm. You have a framework to regain control.

Time management is now a well-developed science with a respectable body of literature of its own. Applied to amateur gardening, though, a few simple guidelines will do very well.

Step 1

Make a master list of the jobs that need to be done in the garden for a month at a time or, at the most, for a season. Trying to plan for the whole year, except in the most general terms, is too daunting, and you won't do it. The list should begin with the most urgent chores. Jobs that you've been dreading should also have priority.

Step 2

This should be done some time before each gardening stint; the evening before if you garden every day or Friday night if you're a weekends only gardener. Take the first item on the list and break it down into smaller steps. List them.

For example: 'Mulch the garden beds' becomes:

Mulch
1. front beds
2. side beds
3. back garden

'Prune the roses' becomes:

Prune
1. *climbers*
2. *standards*
3. *bushes*

Step 3

Head straight for the first job on your list, looking neither to right nor left in case you see something else that is shrieking for attention. Once you get down to work, forget about time altogether. You're dressed for the weather, you have your Walkman playing the 'Pastorale', you're out there for a couple of hours of relaxation. On no account think about finishing the job. You might well finish it, but this is irrelevant. Focus only on the task in hand, work at a slow, measured pace and take pleasure from doing it properly. Pause often to admire your handiwork and relax the muscles in your neck and shoulders. Cultivate a mental image of yourself pottering among the herbs and roses in concert with gardeners through the ages. Rehearse phrases like 'the slow rhythm of the seasons'. Note bees, butterflies, bird calls. It all takes a bit of practice, but it's great therapy.

When you have to stop gardening because of some time constraint, simply stop. Don't start to fret if the job's not finished—there's always another day.

Step 4

As each item on the list is completed, cross it off. This sounds simplistic. It's not; it's very important. The achievement motive is fundamental to the human psyche and the crossing off is a visual confirmation of a task successfully completed. A particular satisfaction is putting a firm line through a job you've been putting off for ages. This simple strategy is surprisingly effective even for those who imagine themselves to be far too old and cynical for such infantile tricks. It even works for those who purvey them.

Step 5
Review of progress. The modus operandi outlined in Steps 1–4 certainly makes for peaceful and relaxed gardening. But the possibility of a major glitch developing in the system must be admitted. After some time has elapsed, the gardener may find himself contemplating a beautifully cultivated and manicured corner while the rest of the allotment resembles an illustration from 'Sleeping Beauty'. Not a soothing sight to the beholder.

And so to the next principle of stress-free gardening. If you cannot keep pace with the requirements of your garden in an enjoyable fashion, you must change it.

1. Make a list of the most time-consuming recurring chores.
2. Work out a way of eliminating or reducing them.
For example:
Problem—lawn care.
   Solution—replace lawns with paving.
Problem—weeding flower beds.
   Solution—replace flower beds with lawn/paving.
Problem—watering.
   Solution—install sprinkler system.
Problem—doing the annuals.

Gardening and Stress

Solution—use perennials.
Problem—doing the perennials.
Solution—use shrubs.
Problem—too much area.
Solution—sell the house; you can lavish infinite time and care on a small courtyard or a windowbox.

What you don't put on your list are the things you really enjoy doing, like potting the orchids or hybridising new roses, no matter how time consuming these may be. After all, this is what it's all about. But everything else should be closely scrutinised. With a little ingenuity and a willingness to consider drastic solutions, it is surprisingly easy to rationalize most areas of the garden to reduce the dreadful feeling that things are getting away from you.

I rest my case with a quotation from an impeccable authority:

> *I do not envy owners of very large gardens. The garden should fit its master or his tastes just as his clothes do; it should be neither too large or too small, but just comfortable. If the garden is larger than he can individually garden and plan and look after, then he is no longer its master but its slave, just as surely as the much-too-rich man is the slave and not the master of his superfluous wealth.*
>
> GERTRUDE JEKYLL, 'WOOD AND GARDEN'.

ACCEPTING LIMITATIONS

One of the cornerstones of stress management is the dictum which runs 'Worry only about those things you can control'.

This excellent piece of advice is as relevant to the garden as anywhere else. Take, for example, the dilemma of trees in the small city garden. On the one hand, it is highly desirable to screen out unedifying views like a block of flats or the neighbours' clothesline. As a screen, trees are without question the most beautiful option. Even if the views over the fence are unexceptional, the impression of privacy and enclosure that trees can furnish is valuable to the residents of a crowded city. On the other hand, trees are enormously greedy for light, water and nutriment, taking a lion's share of these essential ingredients in a small garden. A decision must be taken as to the relative importance of privacy and garden space for smaller plants. This will require careful thought. But once a decision has been made for trees instead of, say, high trellis, the gardener must accept that it is a waste of time to try to do the double. The vast majority of smaller plant such as roses and perennials will not do well close to large trees. It is futile to fight against this. If you want the tree, accept that it has to have its territory. Try a hardy ground cover, maybe, but leave it at that.

By the same token, it is wise to accept that one can't control climate or, to a large degree, soil. Why try to grow avocados in Melbourne or roses in Cairns? Don't hanker after rhododendrons in your lime-ridden plot, or at least don't plant them. It will do your ulcers no good at all.

Eustress vs Distress

To finish on an 'up-note', it would be well to point out that there is a positive as well as a negative side to stress. In the jargon of the trade, positive stress is called eustress, a term which as yet could not be said to be a household word. Eustress, the opposite of distress, is the feeling of exhilaration that comes from pleasurable stimulation and increased adrenalin activity. People seek this type of stress when they engage in pastimes like gambling and parachute jumping. Now it is unlikely that this sort of buzz will be a daily phenomenon in the garden. But there is a source of stimulation and excitement to be had from gardening, as distinct from the relaxation generally associated with the pastime. I refer of course to change.

Seasonal change and development—growth, budding, flowering, fruiting—are constant features of the garden and generate their own pleasure and, at times, excitement. But for real galvanism, nothing can touch a total revamp of the design. Unfortunately, a complete re-modelling is thumpingly expensive and laborious, something to be undertaken once or twice in a lifetime, if at all. But minor thrill-seeking is feasible somewhat more frequently. Winter is a good time for this exercise in morale boosting. Consider which bit of the garden worries or bores you most. Get out all your gardening books. Buy or borrow some new ones. Comb through them for the inspiration which will transform that drab corner into a joy forever. Reject no option at once, no matter how exotic. There is much fun to be had from toying with numerous diverse schemes, positioning structures, plants and ornaments in your mind until you hit on a combination that rings the bell to send you scurrying to the catalogues in a state of high excitement. Who needs to leap out of aeroplanes?

GUIDELINES FOR
STRESS-FREE GARDENING

1. Be comfortable while you work. Consciously relax. Spoil yourself a little. Work to a plan or system, no matter how sketchy.
2. Focus on one small job at a time, concentrating on enjoying it.
3. If the volume of work is too great to cope with enjoyably, reduce it by any means at your disposal.
4. Accept limitations of climate and site.
5. Remove or move all failures with all speed.
6. Stimulate your interest by frequently planning, and sometimes making, changes and improvements. Sit down with a large drink and admire your handiwork.

STATUS
QUO

*T*he logical finishing point for this memoir would appear to be a statement of sorts as to what I have learned in the long trial-and-error process which is its subject. The short answer is probably not much. The impressive depth of my ignorance was brought home to me as recently as last year. An article written by another amateur gardener for a prestigious journal was introduced with the modest disclaimer that before taking up gardening, the author didn't know a daphne from a diosma. Now a daphne I could place. The rest had me stumped. If this is some sort of standard literacy test for beginners, I don't seem to have progressed very far along the learning curve.

However, a miscellany of facts and opinions based for the most part on bitter experience has accumulated over the years, and I see no good reason not to burden you with some of it in the best traditions of books of this sort.

*L*EARNING THE *B*ASICS

An odd place for a heading like this, you may think, at the end of the book. But it is a curious fact that it's possible to 'garden' off and on for twenty years and only begin to come to grips with the fundamentals of the game at the end of that time. It is difficult to think of another case where this is so. You can't play any sport without acquiring the basic skills, can't knit if you don't know the stitches, can't play bridge without knowing the cards. Yet many amateur gardeners go on for years pushing plants into the ground in a hopeful sort of a way without knowing the first thing about soil conditioning, correct watering and feeding or pest and disease control. My own career is a classic example.

However, in the last few years a new spirit of enquiry has been abroad in the land. One encounters old friends rushing off to lectures at horticultural college or fretting about the overdue essay on the biology of earthworms. Now this is an excellent thing. I have no doubt that formal instruction for me would be to the great benefit of my garden. The problem is that my enrolling in another course of any description would spark an armed uprising on the domestic front. My children still break out in a rash if they see me with a clipboard. So my efforts in the direction of practising good horticulture remain in the do-it-yourself category.

One principle that I finally have a firm grip on is the fundamental importance of the soil. Conditioning the soil is becoming a bit of an obsession. The business of making compost not infrequently takes people this way, I've noticed. Fired with conserving zeal I purchased, at considerable expense, a chopping machine and two enormous plastic bins. Every pruning, every orange peel was meticulously shredded and tenderly bedded down with layers of soil, blood and bone, hoof and horn and a few sheets of Saturday's classifieds for good measure. My compost was accelerated with packets of organicness and tested for temperature. Worms were introduced. The thought of that rich hoard of warm brown goodies kept me going all through that winter.

Came time for the spring mulch. I sank the first spade into

the dark manna. It was a solid mass of elm roots. The old warrior, scarcely able to believe its luck, had made the most of the unexpected feast on its doorstep. Bowing to the inevitable, we have left the bins there as the elm's larder and throw in the grass clippings and some fertilizer from time to time. The old tree needs all the help it can get. Compost continues to come in bags as it has always done. It seems cheaper than buying the house next door to get away from the elm.

Grappling with various pests and diseases is also occupying an increasing amount of my time. I have discovered that the catalogue of plant and soil diseases is long and gruesome. Frustrated by recurring casualties, I bought a book with the arresting title 'What Garden Pest or Disease is That?'. A more repellent picture book would be hard to find. Pictures of foul decay and grotesque excrescence are captioned with a succession of names from the Dark Ages to strike fear into the hearts of the ungodly: blight, blotch, canker, club-root, gall, gangrene, mould, rot, scab, slime. One is only surprised not to find plague. Shaken, I hastily closed the book, devoutly thankful not to be afflicted with the worst of the lot—the scourge that lurks beneath the mild, even attractive sobriquet of honey or cinnamon fungus. Those obscene outcroppings of brown doom regularly erupt in several gardens of my acquaintance, but so far my garden has escaped, possibly because I firmly refuse all kind offers of plants and swab down my shoes after a visit. Mildew and black spot, however, I have in abundance. Spraying with Triforine has become a necessity rather than an optional extra. But how to persuade oneself to remember to do it regularly?

It was the pest section of the book, though, that forced the realization that this is a very crowded planet. The mystery is that any plant survives at all. There are over a million species of insects and, despite large-scale intensive chemical warfare, man has not come even close to eliminating one of them. Gives pause for thought, doesn't it? Some gardeners eschew the unequal struggle and leave the arthropoda to get on with their ceaseless internecine warfare. I suspect that most, like me, conduct a futile guerilla campaign which achieves at best a temporary and incomplete respite for the plants. I tend to use middle-range weapons like Malathion. Soft options like soapy water and garlic sprays simply don't work for me and the heavies like Rogor or Dieldrin frighten the living daylights out of me.

Other garden nuisances like defecating dogs and spraying tomcats don't even rate a mention in this aforementioned and massive tome. And what about birds? I have seen plenty of advice on how to encourage our feathered friends, but precious little on how to discourage their significant vandalism in the garden. The loss of all soft fruit I am resigned to—after all, this is not subsistence farming. But what drives me nuts is their instant dispersal of layers of precious compost and manure so carefully applied to beds and borders. Blackbirds are the worst offenders—they follow in the footsteps of the unsuspecting spreader, joyfully scratching and digging and scattering all his good work to the four winds, frequently uprooting seedlings and small plants in the process. An effective deterrent was not easy to find. Patent humming wires didn't work, a silhouette of a hawk was ignored after ten minutes and around here bird nets are *verboten*. In desperation, I retrieved the banished nets and cut them into long strips. Cackling shrilly, I skewered the strips along the edges of all the beds and borders with long hairpins. Hallelujah. The blackbirds, having got their toes caught up in the fine black netting once or twice, retreated to consider the problem. It's hell getting the weeds out through the mesh, though.

But all these slings and arrows are as nothing compared with that species which remains the bane, the bugbear, the *grande bête noire* of my gardening life, the possum. All the preventatives, the traps, spells and incantations referred to earlier in this narrative have been equally useless. Still we wake in fright as they thunder across over our heads; still the buds and green shoots disappear in the night. In one last despairing fling, I have wheeled in a new weapon. The fence tops and the rose arbour are currently adorned with several brand-new strands of barbed wire. In a largely unsuccessful attempt to soften the effect of a smaller Stalag come to the suburbs, the wire has been painted Brunswick green. We must have the only designer barbed wire in the country. Broken in spirit by countless defeats, I am deeply pessimistic about its effectiveness. We can only hunch down in our bunker and wait.

FAVOURITE PLANTS

I love to read catalogues of other people's favourite plants and so am encouraged to compile my own very arbitrary list. Selection is heavily weighted in favour of plants of neat and restrained habit as being most suited to the small city garden. And they are, above all, survivors.

Trees

Eucalyptus gunnii: This tree may well be more popular in Europe than in its country of origin. It is prized in the northern hemisphere for its beautiful juvenile foliage— intriguing disc-shaped leaves of a striking blue-grey. The tree appears quite happy to be annually prevented from reaching maturity, pruned to a round graceful shrub of about two metres.

Juniperus virginiana: 'Skyrocket'. A slender conifer which has many merits. The colour is an attractive blue-grey which, in certain lights and especially in autumn, can take on an almost luminous appearance. The tree never becomes thick of girth and does not grow to great heights. Estimates of mature height vary quite a lot, but the majority opinion seems to be around 5–6 metres. The root system is fine and does not pose problems for walls or paving. I have seen a row of Skyrockets looking quite sensational growing along the side of a blue-grey house.

Dwarf Peach: Not much larger than a shrub, these loveable little trees grow tidily to a metre or so and provide good foliage contrast in a mixed border. They look particularly good with roses. On my trees the leaves (a strong pendulous shape) are more attractive than the flowers which are an unfortunate shade variously described as knicker pink or toothpaste pink. One could add bubblegum pink. But happily the flowers don't last long. (There are other varieties, one of which has white flowers.) The fruit incidentally is quite good to eat.

Crab Apple (Malus) 'Gorgeous': How could you resist the name? The white flowers of this smaller growing crab apple are perhaps not as spectacular as some of the tribe, but the fruits are a delight—bright red, and held on the tree for quite a long period.

Shrubs

Roses: Just why this single genus of the plant kingdom has throughout history exercised such fascination, excited such passionate devotion and elicited such quantities of admiring, not to say gushing poetry and prose, is not entirely clear. Certainly no one would dispute that roses are very beautiful. But other plants produce equally beautiful and, in fact, very similar flowers. Paeonies, for instance, and camellias. These, of course, have their devotees also, but they are paltry tribes compared to the vast hordes of roses fanciers. And, like all prima donnas, roses make their admirers pay dearly for their passion. What other plant in your garden requires the year-round intensive care regime demanded by roses before they will give of their best? Pruning, feeding, spraying with a vast array of medications, watching for, and invariably finding, signs of pest or disease; life is not easy for a rose lover. Having said that, I must own to being a paid-up, card-carrying member of the rose fan club. I have planted far too many, yearn for those I can't fit in and order more every year knowing there's no room. Disappointment has been frequent. Any rose that looks like a poor doer runs a grave danger of being yanked out to make way for some new paragon which promises more. If I left well enough alone and let them get on with it, the results I know would be better, but I seem to be a compulsive interventionist.

Another cause of lacklustre performance has been, I feel sure, my over-use of under-planting. 'Roses need company' Christopher Lloyd instructs briskly and, as always, he is absolutely right. During my daily walks through the Botanic Gardens I have over the last few years conducted a rough survey not only of good all-season performers and combinations but also of sights that affront and offend. I hasten to add that the former category is immensely larger than the latter, but even in these magnificent public gardens there are one or two real shockers. The rose beds in the-off season are at the top of my black-list, beating home that other strong contender, the island bed of mixed cannas. So, in a small garden especially, a roses-only bed is not an attractive proposition. Mixed beds it must be. Running true to form, I planted *all* the companion plants suggested by assorted gurus. The young rose bushes were engulfed in burgeoning clumps of cranesbills, Japanese anemones, campanulas, verbenas, irises, alchemilla mollis, anthemis, garlic, violas and a host of other friends and relations. If a rose appeared at all through all of this, it looked like a distress flare.

A current project is the removal or drastic curtailing of most of the inhabitants of the precious sunny beds. My irrational bias in favour of the roses has spelled the end for many of the hapless companions which actually looked very pretty. I only hope the roses respect the sacrifice and do the right thing next season. Some have already proved themselves good performers despite the tough opposition.

'Iceberg'. The Iceberg phenomenon rolls on and on. As Dr James Hitchmough observed recently, 'In parts of Melbourne, ['Iceberg'] is so ubiquitous that overseas visitors might easily believe that it was the State's floral emblem'. One feels apologetic about planting it. Garden visitors will exclaim 'What is that wonderful rose? Oh, it's (only) "Iceberg"', as if it were cheating in some way to have it there at all. If I think I can get away with it, I have been known to say that it's 'Schneewittchen', impressing the hell out of the uninitiated who would have dismissed the efforts of common old 'Iceberg'. I certainly have nothing to equal it in my garden for performance, and have a great fondness for it. On the shortest day of this year, admittedly after a long mild autumn, all my 'Icebergs' were in flower. On the largest bush there were fifty-one flowers or buds showing colour.

'Ballerina'. As a group, Reverend Pemberton's Hybrid Musks are hard to beat, even up against the best that modern hybridizers can produce. The bushes are actually attractive in a generous, blowsy sort of way. They do use quite a lot of that precious commodity, space, but even in a small garden, one of the Hybrid Musks will give worthwhile returns in length of flowering season and abundance of blooms. I like them all very much, but would choose 'Ballerina' for the ingenuous charm of its small single pink-and-white flowers produced in great numbers.

'Chaucer'. One of David Austin's prodigies. The bush is unremarkable, growing to about a metre, but the flowers! Pale, translucent pink with the petals forming a perfect cup, this is the 'cabbage' rose of your dreams. Current holder of my personal 'most beautiful rose' award.

'Radox Bouquet'. A recent hybrid tea of considerable merit saddled with a truly dreadful name. Where do they find them? It sounds like an athletic linament. The flowers are a clear and lively pink, deeper at the centre, and in my garden are produced in successive flushes over a very long period, right into winter. While the bush is modern in its gawkiness, the flowers have a distinctly 'old-fashioned' appearance, making this rose a very good standby for cheats. I have three bushes and a standard.

For the purists, it may be of interest to pass on my observations over a number of years of walking past the 'Old Rose' beds in the Botanic Gardens, which contain a fair range of the genuine article. The two best performers have been 'Lamarque', which has a very long flowering season, and the curious Mutabilis (*Rosa chinensis mutabilis*) which is still displaying its intriguing multi-coloured blooms long after most of the oldies have reverted to an ugly tangle of sticks. I like Mutabilis a lot, but it grows to quite a big bush—almost two metres tall and as wide—so is perhaps a luxury for the small garden.

Camellias: What more could you ask of a shrub than a camellia offers, year in and year out, in a reliable and uncomplaining way? Glossy evergreen foliage, a wide range of flower types to suit every taste from the big-is-vulgar to the bigger-the-better school, shade tolerance, great beauty and the rudest of health. Add to that the fact that their flowering season spans the dullest time in the gardening year and you have an impressive claim to popularity. So I am more than a little mystified as to why the genus is largely ignored by English gardeners, or at least by English garden writers. In that seminal work of haute culture, 'The Englishwoman's Garden', camellias didn't rate a single mention. The only entry on camellias in the equally patrician 'Englishman's Garden' is a reference to the garden owned by Mr Fred Nutbeam, gardener to the nobility. What could it be about this admirable shrub that offends the sensibilities of persons of taste and refinement? What subtle vulgarity had escaped my untutored eye? Rhododendrons and azaleas appear to attract a similar odium, relegated for the most part to the decent concealment of the spinney or wood. This worried me for a while. Should I avoid camellias altogether, being a bit light on woods? I am a very insecure gardener. Common-sense won a rare victory—camellias are the perfect shrub for the small garden, looking attractive at all times, and giving much pleasure during their long flowering season. I now have many of them and wouldn't be without any, particularly the sasanquas, which look so fragile and are as tough as old boots.

If camellias are not everywhere as popular as they deserve to be, perhaps those who choose the names should accept some of the blame. Two of my favourites rejoice in the names 'Dr Tinsley' and 'E.G. Waterhouse'. Really sing to you, don't they? Another treasure is called 'Cinnamon Cindy' which I'm not sure is any better. How about 'Widdle Wun' (sic)? Or 'Richard Nixon', for heaven's sake? Some beautiful plants have been dealt a cruel blow by their creators.

Personal Bests

Best tub specimen: *Camellia japonica 'Magnoliiflora'* (syn. Hagoromo). Delicate pale pink 'hose-in-hose' form, this japonica grows happily in a pot for years, forming a well-shaped bush with leaves that are not too big.

Best garden performer: 'E.G. Waterhouse' (Williamsii hybrid). An Australian hybrid, this large shrub has attractive smallish foliage and clear pink formal double flowers. In my garden it has proved amazingly tolerant of dry conditions. It is also mercifully self-grooming, as the bushes quickly grow too tall to deadhead easily. Few sights are as unappealing as a camellia covered in mushy brown corpses.

Best sasanqua: 'Apple Blossom' (syn. 'Fukuzutsumi', 'Zerbes'). Fragile-looking pink and white single. Also very drought resistant and espaliers well.

Best foliage: *'Camellia lutchuensis'*. Small pointed leaves, sometimes red-tipped. This species of camellia has the added bonus of small single white flowers with a distinct sweet scent.

Philadelphus: This group of mock oranges seems to be included in most must-have lists. And quite rightly so. They make big graceful arching shrubs with attractive foliage and wonderfully scented flowers. In Australia they often retain their leaves throughout the winter. I like them all, but find that 'Virginal' and 'Grandiflorus' grow too big for my garden. *Philadelphus mexicanus* has the most graceful cascading growing habit.

Box *(Buxus sempervirens)*: My feelings about this simple evergreen are somewhat complex. On one level I am passionate about it, deriving great satisfaction from the clipping and trimming of this accommodating plant into precise shapes which give me renewed pleasure every time I pass. Recently, though, it has occurred to me that perhaps we are entering a phase of Buxus overload. No smart garden centre could open its doors without an array of box balls and lollipops in the obligatory Italian pot. Every garden with any claims to distinction has its meticulously clipped box hedges or, if the budget was a bit tight, rows of little box plants growing as fast as they can towards their first tonsure. Occasionally the thought crosses my mind that this can't be right; that box is surely a quintessentially English plant, wildly inappropriate in the land of ghost gums and kangaroo paws. So far, these uneasy stirrings are pushed aside readily enough—there aren't too many ghost gums in inner Melbourne after all—and I happily resume urging on the embryonic double poodle standard in the Vatican courtyard. But a recent article in an American magazine made me falter for a moment. One Massachusetts nursery alone sold 10,000 box topiaries in the last twelve months. Topiary enthusiasts were interviewed. The wife of one captain of industry was a dedicated practitioner: 'I find topiary a wonderful challenge. I just love to make plants look the way they shouldn't.' Alexander Pope, where are you?

My Four Best Greys

French Lavender *(Lavandula dentata)*: Altogether a more phlegmatic type than the rest of the tribe, my French lavender looks good and flowers for most of the year. Better still, its woolly grey mound stoutly resists the craze for self-immolation which afflicts so many of its English cousins.

Cushion Bush *(Calocephalus brownii)*: An Australian native with bright silver-white finely cut foliage which looks very like coral. The intensity of the silver makes this bush a marvellous foil for almost any flower. It looks particularly good with pink roses. Older plants seem to lose their purity of colour which is not really restored by cutting back. It's better to start again with a new bush. Heaven knows how these curious plants are propagated—they look quite inanimate to me.

Santolina: I have tried two varieties; the first called, I think, *Santolina incana* I had no luck with at all. It was a small-leaved variety which was very prone to mildew and die-back. I now have several bushes of the larger-leaved *Santolina chamaecyparissus* which seems much hardier. It has fine feathery foliage and is easily kept to a pleasing shape.

Curry Plant *(Helichrysum angustifolium)*: Tolerant of drought, easy to prune, it accepts the loss of its rather boring yellow flowers with equanimity. Another good grey-silver mound.

These four all grow to around one metre or less and are not rampageous by nature, although the roots of *Calocephalus brownii* have to be watched.

Perennials
Chinese Foxglove *(Rhemannia angulata)*: Looking

rather like a dwarf pink foxglove, these evergreen perennials are worth including for length of flowering season. With adequate water and a bit of encouragement in the way of feeding, they will flower from spring to late autumn.

Artemesia frigida: Apparently there is some confusion about the name of this uncommon perennial. It is worth looking for. The silvery foliage is fine and lacy and the flower spikes resemble those of small verbascums. The flowers are yellow, but they take a long time to open and are easy to remove if they are the ruination of your colour scheme.

***Geranium endressi* 'Wargrave Pink':** This true geranium forms a neat clump of rounded leaves and small five-petalled flowers of gelati-pink. Not to be confused with the strident magenta 'Russell Pritchard'.

Iris sibirica: Good tidy clumps of slender green spears and small beardless flowers of bright blue or white, I have found it agreeably adaptable to a wide range of conditions.

Lychnis flos-jovis: A lower-growing relative of *Lychnis coronaria*, the foliage is looser and more inclined to spread. It is mid silver-grey in colour and an agreeable contrast to the clear rose-pink flowers which appear all during the summer and autumn.

Herbs

Rue *(Ruta graveolens)*: For years I have searched without success for the variety of rue called 'Jackman's Blue', recommended by every writer who ever mentions the herb.

I have seen it described as iridescent blue, striking blue, rich blue, true blue. It seems generally held to be quite blue. As far as I can ascertain it hasn't reached Melbourne, so I have yet to clap eyes on this cerulean cultivar. My plant is just plain rue but it still makes a neat pretty bush with a bluish cast to the foliage.

Purple Sage: The soft grey/purple/green of the foliage makes this plant an excellent foil for paler flowering shrubs, particularly those with pale pink flowers. Its greatest flaw is a tendency to suddenly succumb to some mysterious blight which causes severe wilting and die-back. I tend to treat it as an annual.

Garlic chives *(Allium tuberosum)*: These form attractive clumps of narrow flat leaves about 40 centimetres high and, in late summer, round heads of star-shaped white flowers which are held high above the foliage. They have a better garden effect than the common chive (*A. schoenoprasum*) which is a much smaller plant.

Bush Basil *(Ocimum minimum)*: This seems a relatively uncommon herb. I have found it only once and it grew into a very handsome purple-tinged bush about half a metre tall. Unsure of its requirements, I decided it looked like a perennial and cut it back hard in the autumn. It promptly died. I regret its loss very much and still look for it in nurseries.

None of these herbs do we actually eat. Rue smells vile, the green sage looks safer than the purple, both the garlic chives and the bush basil are too strongly flavoured for me. But then, as an old acquaintance of mine once observed on downing her third gin-and-water, 'It's not the taste dear, it's the effect that counts'.

Ground covers

A contentious subject among garden writers. One group appears to regard the use of ground covers as not quite cricket, and makes disparaging remarks about heather or lamiums. Those sages who do recommend their use nevertheless pepper their prose with adjectives like 'thuggish'. I do see their point. My first all-purpose ground cover was the mock strawberry, duchesnia. Pretty as it was, it finally had to go. The plant spreads by throwing out long runners and, if conditions are to its liking, can leap tall buildings at a single bound. The whole garden was disappearing in a tidal wave of duchesnia. I still have it in pots. It foams luxuriously from around the base of three standard camellias in large tubs and very nice they look too. But duchesnia's thuggishness has made me much more wary of ground covers. An experiment with *Cerastium tomentosum* was equally unsuccessful. It looks beautiful but is very invasive. Rather than use plants that spread rapidly, I now favour low-growing perennials which serve the same soil-covering, weed-smothering function, but do not have hegemonous tendencies.

Potentilla nepalensis, v. 'Miss Willmott': I regard this as a great find. The leaves and flowers are very like that of a strawberry, and this variety has beguiling strawberry pink blooms with a small red eye. Each plant will grow to around 20 centimetres in height and cover about one square metre.

Alpine strawberry *(Fragaria vesca):* These mix very well with the Potentilla, forming neat little clumps which look endearing and never give any trouble. They seem much less subject to mould than ordinary strawberries and do not seek to colonize by runners.

Rosa 'Snow Carpet': A tiny rose with dense glossy foliage on prostrate miniature canes, it produces its small white flowers for quite a long period in spring and summer. Spreading to about half a metre, it is almost evergreen and doesn't require much in the way of pruning.

'Maiden pink' *(Dianthus deltoides):* Dense cushions of fine dark green foliage which will trail gracefully over a wall or path. The flowers are quite a strong deep pink, but are so tiny that they are not overpowering. There is a white variety, *Dianthus deltoides alba*, but in my garden this has proved rather a puny specimen.

WHAT'S IT ALL ABOUT?

At the risk of sounding hackneyed, I have to say that the most important lesson I have learnt from all this is that gardening is an unfailing source of immense and continuing pleasure. While this is hardly a novel conclusion, it is worth stating in view of the chronicle of misadventure which has just passed before your eyes. Because one of the great joys of gardening is that when something goes wrong, as it very frequently does, it is almost always possible to fix it. This simple fact is an enormous comfort to the amateur, whose aspirations are rarely matched by reality. If you sit down and think, really think, about a problem area or planting, some ugliness that must somehow be screened or some re-arrangement which will be more pleasing, you will eventually hit on a solution which will send you leaping from your bath to begin the exciting work of transformation, ensuring an increased flow of adrenalin into the system and readies out of the bank account. The best days for a gardener are those on which a new project is launched. Anticipation is all. Never mind the disappointment which is bound to be lurking around the corner; you can always fix that too.

This means, of course, that the plants of a passionate gardener are in a more or less continuously mobile state, bundled from one spot to another like the furniture or paintings. I don't think this does them much harm, though some of the grouchier daphnes and clematis object strenuously. For the most part I choose to regard the re-arranging as therapeutic; it keeps them on their toes. I read somewhere a comment by the talented actor-turned-gardener Reg Livermore on his spectacular display of daffodils; it was the first year he hadn't moved them and they were hysterical with relief. The odds are long that they are still in the same spot. The true addict can never stop experimenting.

There are times, though, when gardening is much more enjoyable than at others. The joys of spring are well documented and any further eulogizing from me would be tedious. The other seasons are a bit of a mixed bag. At first mystified to learn that Vita Sackville-West made a practice of leaving Sissinghurst for long periods during the summer, I now understand perfectly. Late summer is the most unsettling time of the year. Rampant, indecent growth greets the eye on every side; all is blowsy, overblown, over the top. The sooner the work of restoring order with the autumn cutting back begins, the better. Autumn is a splendid time for the gardener. All that satisfying activity—uprooting and pruning, buying of new plants, the creating of new compost and the spreading of old. Very Tabitha Twitchett. But I'm not sure that winter isn't actually the season I like best (which is something of a worry in itself). That threatening, multiplying growth out there is cowed, reigned back, neat and trim, in control. Light floods in. Clean lines can be discerned. And grand plans and wondrous projects, spurred on by the perfidious catalogues, burgeon and bloom in the mind's eye with a far greater splendour than ever has been seen in one small garden.

And what of style? I suffered one or two dark (well, dimmish) nights of the soul when I realized that my little parterre, so firmly and permanently bricked in, was not a fresh and original concept in this country at all, but part of the latest wave of fashion. This should have come as no surprise. The conditioning process goes on and who am I to gainsay Pavlov? But the fact that I manage time after time to wake up in the middle of a trend is a little irksome. In the case of gardening at least it's in the middle; I have long since learned that as I become aware of a fashion in clothing, this is an unerring indicator that the look is as dead as a dodo.

But disillusionment with my vogue-ish front garden didn't really last long. I realized pretty smartly that faddish or not, derivative or not, I really do like it. I potter round happily for hours on end, enjoying the feeling of being secluded, protected, cloistered. Many before me have felt the same way; this form of enclosed, orderly gardening has been comforting the timid human spirit for centuries. Just why it is enjoying such a strong revival now is not altogether clear. Descended from the medieval cloister, the style found particular favour in far-flung colonies like the early American settlements. Informed opinion has it that the traditional formal enclosed gardens of the early settlers (notably the Dutch) were a reaction against the immense and hostile wilderness which surrounded them. Many early Australian gardens were similarly carefully geometric and enclosed. It is not unreasonable to suppose that our instinct to impose order on the environment is strongest when such order is under greatest threat.

In the late twentieth century, the hazards in one's immediate surroundings are not as readily apparent. Attacks from wild beasts or hostile natives are relatively rare events in the suburbs these days. The move towards high-walled gardens and formality in arrangement is perhaps a response to the more subtle pressures of overcrowding, future shock or dim fears of a global *Gotterdamerung*. Jeanne Larmoth, writing in 'American House and Garden' put it very well. (She was actually writing about the enthusiasm for old-fashioned pinks or dianthus, but her comments are equally relevant to the whole English garden trend).

Painting the Roses White

The reason for [the traditional English garden's] return to fashion at this point is much the same as the reason that chintz flourishes in the living room and the Cavalier King Charles spaniel on the hearth; the sense of security, there for the borrowing, built into the British tradition.

Whatever the cause, nostalgia rides high in current garden design and I suspect will ride even higher before we move on to fresh horizons. A distinctive Australian style of greater complexity than the railway sleepers and native-plants-only variety will undoubtedly evolve over time, and a very good thing too. In the meantime, or even in the thereafter, there is no reason at all why you shouldn't buy and plant just whatever you fancy. The gardeners I admire most are those of genuinely catholic taste. I am trying to cultivate this in myself. I have taken to stopping in my walks to study things like golden conifers, orange flowers, cacti, agaves and yuccas, striving for an open mind. Success has not been immediate, but I did detect a faint warming to a variegated agave the other day. Which probably means that we're about to be swamped in a tidal wave of agaves and that they have, in fact, been the *dernier cri* for the last twelve months.

But at long last, I am inching towards the confidence necessary to plant what I want and to hell with it. And whether this happens to be 'in', 'out' or unheard of, it will not mean the end of Western civilization as we know it. The best gardening advice I ever read came from Sir Frederick Ashton:

Status Quo

*M*y advice to a beginner would be 'Do exactly what you want to do, and don't listen to anybody . . . Put in the plants you like. And if you like those terrible red salvias then put them in.'

Now *there's* an idea.

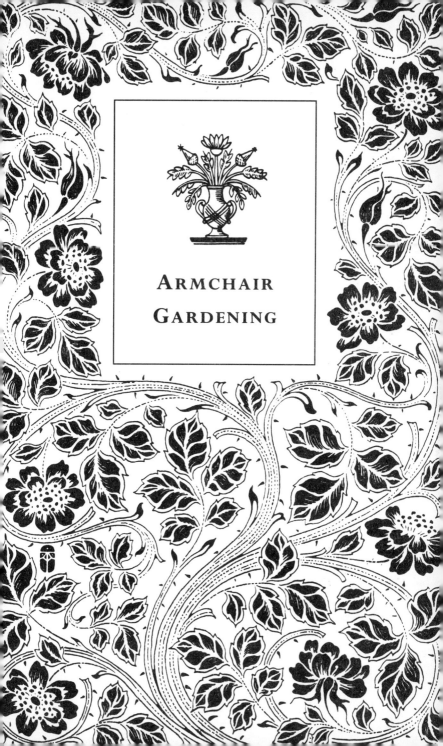

ARMCHAIR
GARDENING

*W*hile most of my reading on gardening has been in quest of enlightenment, I have been delighted to find that some writers afford much entertainment by way of bonus.

The following collection of wit, wisdom and one-liners has been compiled in a haphazard fashion over a number of years. It does seem rather biased towards English writers. This may reflect the limited scope of my reading as much as anything else. Australia has a sizeable coterie of highly articulate garden writers and I feel sure that lurking somewhere in America there is a whole covey of coruscating scriveners, a sort of horticultural Algonquin Round Table, that I dream of one day discovering. But it may also be that the English authors are writing from a position of such strength and assurance that they have the confidence not to take themselves or their art too seriously.

It takes confidence to write with this degree of candour:

> *O*ne of the things that keeps me enthusiastic is competition. I go round other people's gardens with a jealous eye. I see someone's roses growing without a touch of blackspot (one of my many banes) and feel sick with envy. What makes me a really happy woman is to go round some garden that is wrongly constructed, planted in bad taste and rather untidy. I am then extraordinarily civil to

Painting the Roses White

the owner, say how beautiful everything is and go home in a highly contented state of mind.

THE LADY CAROLINE SOMERSET IN 'THE ENGLISHWOMAN'S GARDEN'.

Or this:

Those squat little figures sitting on rockeries are not always gnomes. Some of them are conifers, doing duty. Most such are man-selected, not known in the wild, and doubtless they reflect man's hopes and aspirations in some kinky way. 'They provide full stops and vertical accents', you will be told by those sufficiently articulate to put such clap-trap into words (I do it myself, but then it's different).

CHRISTOPHER LLOYD, 'THE WELL-CHOSEN GARDEN'.

I feel impelled at this point to pay tribute to Mr Christopher Lloyd, though that worthy gentleman must get heartily sick of such panegyrics. A good deal of whatever gardening wisdom I have acquired comes from his books, and a most painless process it has been. Mr Lloyd emerges from his writing as a skilful and dedicated gardener with a vast store of practical knowledge and a most winning way with words. You were quite pleased with your white garden?

White flowers show up particularly well on a shady aspect and the large white clematis 'Marie Boisselot' is excellent here. You might combine it with the vigorous white-flowering climbing rose, 'Mme Alfred Carriere', well-known as a successful north waller. White with white is terribly chic, didn't you know? Oh but, my dear, you cannot expect white flowers to do themselves justice except in a white milieu. And

182

the walls should be white, too. A symphony in white. There
are so many shades of white; an infinity of nuances. Such
a pity we cannot do away with all those green leaves.
CHRISTOPHER LLOYD, 'THE WELL-TEMPERED GARDEN'.

Excesses of fashion are attacked somewhat more passionately
by that very good garden writer of an earlier generation,
Reginald Farrer:

It is the grief of humanity that from one extreme of
error it must always sway back into another . . . In
gardening we are now enduring the backwash of just such a
terrific wave, whose recession down the naked shingles of the
world leaves our horticultural future rather doubtful . . . But
suddenly (after the excesses of the Victorian era) there comes
a Moses to our need. Out of the dense darkness arises the
immortal Mr Robinson, pointing the way to escape. He
reminds us of beauties which we had almost forgotten and
leads us on to a land flowing with sweetness and delight. Yet
all these emancipations have excesses . . . and, in their
contempt for the abuses of the formal system, Mr Robinson's
successors and disciples have been driven into the foolish
extreme of denying all value to form, of insisting on anarchy
in the garden, of declaring that every restraint is hateful. Now
we have nothing but weak lines in our gardens, vague, wibble-
wobble areas that have no meaning nor explanation; our
borders meander up and down and here and there like sheep
that have no shepherd; our silly lawns erupt into silly little
beds like pimples . . . For the prophet's words are always
exaggerated and abused . . . Truth, that unseizable thing,

lies ever between two extremes; and, while the garden of multi-coloured gravel is an offence to the blessed sun, hardly less so is the amorphous foolishness that now makes our borders undulate and flounder so feebly.

REGINALD FARRER, 'MY ROCK GARDEN' IN 'AN ANTHOLOGY OF GARDEN WRITING'.

My favourite of all the earlier writers is undoubtedly E. A. Bowles. He was clearly an immensely erudite gardener. Consider this portrait of a certain obscure lily:

Helicodiceros crinitus is] the most fiendish plant I know of, the sort of thing Beelzebub might pluck to make a bouquet for his mother-in-law . . . [it] looks as if it had been made out of a sow's ear for spathe and the tail of a rat that had died of Elephantiasis for the spadix. The whole thing is a mingling of unwholesome greens, livid purples, and pallid pinks, the livery of putrescence in fact, and it possesses an odour to match the colouring. I once entrapped the vicar of a poor parish into smelling it, and when he had recovered his breath he said it reminded him of a pauper funeral. It only exhales this stench for a few hours after opening, and during that time it is better to stand afar off and look at it through a telescope.

E. A. BOWLES, 'MY GARDEN IN SPRING' IN 'AN ANTHOLOGY OF GARDEN WRITING'.

And this description of a species of crocus:

One little yellow crocus has an obnoxious trait in its character and is a little stinking beast, as Dr Johnson

described the stoat. It is well named *graveolens*, and its heavy
scent is generally the first intimation I get of its having opened
its flowers. Sometimes I get a whiff of it even before I reach
the crocus frame—an abominable mixture of the odour of
black beetles and imitation of skunk, or one of those awful
furs with which people in the next pew or at a matinee poison
you. A dried specimen of this crocus retains its scent for years,
and so does the blotting paper it has been pressed in. I think
it emanates from the pollen grains, and I suppose it must be
of some use to it in its native country—perhaps attractive
to some insect of perverted olfactory tastes.

E. A. BOWLES, 'MY GARDEN IN SPRING' IN 'AN ANTHOLOGY OF
GARDEN WRITING'.

Miss Gertrude Jekyll, an equally distinguished contemporary,
was also no mean wordsmith. While instruction was always
her primary goal, a gentle humour surfaces from time to time.
On one of her pet subjects, colour:

*Finally I paid a visit to the trial-grounds of one of
our premier seed-houses, and saw all the kinds and
colourings and made my own notes. I cannot but think that
a correct description of the colours, instead of a fanciful one,
would help both customer and seed-merchant. The customer,
in order to get the desired flowers, has to learn a code . . .
Thus, if I want a Giant Comet of that beautiful pale silvery
lavender, perhaps the loveliest colour of which a China Aster
is capable, I have to ask for 'azure blue'. If I want a full
lilac, I must order 'blue'; if a full purple, it is 'dark blue'.
If I want a strong rich violet-purple, I must beware of asking*

for purple, for I shall get a terrible magenta such as one year spoilt the whole colour scheme of my Aster garden. It is not as if the right colour-words were wanting, for the language is rich in them—violet, lavender, lilac, mauve, purple; these, with slight additions, will serve to describe the whole of the colouring falsely called blue. The word blue should not be used at all in connection with these flowers. There are no blue China Asters.

GERTRUDE JEKYLL, 'COLOUR SCHEMES FOR THE FLOWER GARDEN'.

The subject of colour in the garden has been addressed by many writers, few of them as entertainingly as Christopher Lloyd:

It is a sad fact that mauve has long been out of favour. 'Women,' wrote Mr Beverley Nichols, 'seem to have come to the conclusion that mauve does something unkind to their complexions. I trust they will not allow this prejudice to extend to the garden.' But emphatically they do. It seems to be not so much the colour that curls them up, as the actual word . . . The word has no pejorative sense to me . . . If it would only stage a comeback, a whole range of garden flowers could share in the bonanza . . . People shy away from mauve as a word but are perfectly content to grow the majority of mauve flowers provided they are discreetly described as lavender or lilac.

CHRISTOPHER LLOYD, 'THE WELL-TEMPERED GARDEN'.

I've settled in the long run for a colour harmony of pinks and mauves rather than a contrasty set-up. I

take this as a sign of advancing years, which is not necessarily
synonymous with maturity.

CHRISTOPHER LLOYD, 'THE WELL-CHOSEN GARDEN'.

nother mistake, easily made by good-natured, kindly
people is to feed your greys, offering them nourishing
dishes of garden compost, farmyard manure, sewage sludge and
such-like delicacies. They are not cut out for this kind of rich
living. Again their leaves will turn green, they'll grow much too
fast making unhealthy, watery shoots and at the first touch of
cold weather, they'll die. It's almost immoral that starvation
should be what they actually thrive on, and I can imagine that
a specialist in greys might become rather a callous, case-hardened
type of person in whom warmth and human sympathy had
withered. He would expect any house guest to exist on dried
peas and soya beans washed down with Arak.

CHRISTOPHER LLOYD, 'THE ADVENTUROUS GARDENER'.

Mr Lloyd has little time for affectation and the good taste
brigade:

re we of the form, texture and delicate colouring school
really such prigs? There is a danger. It is a reaction
to the other extreme that we see in so many front gardens:
the colour addicts who lurch incontinently from lumps of
forsythia and double pink 'Kanzan' cherry, through a blaze
of rhododendrons and dumpy blobs of azalea, floribunda roses,
scarlet salvias and so on to a dying exit with mop-headed
chrysanthemums. That sort of gardening is a bore, especially
as there is so much of it, but at least it is full-bloodedly boring.

Painting the Roses White

> *It wallows in its vulgarity with a sense of enjoyment. The trouble
> with the form-and-texture-and-colour-harmonies gardener is his
> (often her) insufferable self-consciousness.*
>
> CHRISTOPHER LLOYD, 'THE ADVENTUROUS GARDENER'.

It would be advisable to keep one's head well down when
Mr Lloyd picks up his pen. At the same time, though, he is
prepared to be helpful to the beginner, in an astringently
avuncular sort of a way:

> *And so, to the amateur gardener's eternally repeated
> question 'When should I?' and 'What's the best time
> to?' I've concluded that nine times out of ten the answer is 'When
> you're thinking about it; when you're in the mood'. This I realize,
> is the last thing he wants to be told, because it is an adult answer
> and the amateur, in whatever the subject, will long remain a
> child, seeking advice and guide-lines in the form of clear-cut,
> black-or-white answers to his manifold doubts. To be told that it
> doesn't matter is unsettling. The kind answer to 'When should I?'
> is 'Do it on the 31st March.' No shilly-shallying there.*
>
> CHRISTOPHER LLOYD, 'THE WELL-TEMPERED GARDEN'.

I could go on at considerable length, but it would be far better
for you to read Mr Lloyd's books in their entirety. It is a most
rewarding experience.

There are still more delights in this Anglophile anthology.
The aforementioned Mr Beverley Nichols has manifested a
talent to amuse throughout his long writing career. This from
his 1932 best-seller *Down the Garden Path*:

Armchair Gardening

A word about this field. It was three acres of pasture. I was very proud of it. If you stood in the extreme centre of it, and shut one eye, it looked enormous. One had a sense of owning broad acres, and sweating minions, and delicious things like that. However, one could not spend one's time standing in the middle of a field, shutting one eye. People would think it peculiar.

BEVERLEY NICHOLS, 'DOWN THE GARDEN PATH'.

Fifty years later he was writing in 'The Englishman's Garden':

R oses, of course, there are in abundance but these are confined to the walls. But bush roses, no. When they are not flowering, which means the greater part of the year, they are an offence to the eye, meticulously pruned and shaped to a style which bears no relation to anything in Nature. They are hospital cases, from which the eye revolts. Perhaps the most distressing of all are those roses in which flowers of red and yellow are born from the same root.

BEVERLEY NICHOLS IN 'THE ENGLISHMAN'S GARDEN'.

Robin Spencer's introduction to his piece in the same book induced a feeling of instant kinship. The details may differ, but his approach to design I recognized at once:

I n 1977 I changed, somewhat tongue in cheek, our entry in the yellow book 'Gardens Open to the Public in England and Wales' to read 'An owner-made and maintained garden of particular interest to the plantsman, containing orchard with pool, an arbour, miniature pinetum, dell with stream, a Folly, nut walk, peony bed, iris borders, fern border,

> *herb garden, summerhouse, alley, white and silver garden, two*
> *vegetable gardens, and pavement maze all within one acre.'*
> *I added an exclamation mark; but the printer has persistently*
> *omitted it. I often wonder what people expect.*
>
> ROBIN SPENCER IN 'THE ENGLISHMAN'S GARDEN'.

My favourite illustration in this treasured bedtime story book
is a picture of the late Sir David Scott, a sprightly nonagen-
arian, vigorously hoeing at the long grass with a large scythe,
knee pads firmly strapped to his pin-striped knees:

> *ut we could never cope without rubber knee-pads (we*
> *live in them, and the whole garden, except for the*
> *vegetables and fruit, is hand-weeded for the sake of chance*
> *seedlings), a first class mower and a Flymo, as well as a battery*
> *spintrim for the grass edges (if you want to impress visitors,*
> *as every gardener does, keep your edges trimmed), white paint*
> *on the wooden part of all our tools: 'where did your leave the*
> *rubber rake?' 'Over there, can't you see?'—and, to save lengthy*
> *domestic explanations, names for all the beds (some fifty-five*
> *island beds in David's garden alone): 'Where will you be*
> *working this afternoon?' 'In the Barrett border.'*
>
> SIR DAVID SCOTT IN 'THE ENGLISHMAN'S GARDEN'.

The length of his sentences is as much a tribute to his
impressive stamina as were his outdoor activities.

Many writers of garden books seem to be blessed with a
spouse who is companion and soulmate in all their horticultural endeavours. I have at times felt a twinge of envy. But
better, surely, a remote but well-disposed spouse than a
helpmeet like Mr Fish:

Armchair Gardening

*F irmness in all aspects is a most important quality when
gardening, not only in planting but in pruning, dividing
and tying up. Plants are like babies, they know when an
amateur is handling them. My plants knew, but I didn't. Walter
would not tolerate an unhealthy or badly grown plant and if
he saw anything that wasn't looking happy he pulled it up.
Often I would go out and find a row of sick looking plants laid
out like a lot of dead rats. It became something of a game. If
I knew I had an ailing child I was trying to bring round I'd
do my utmost to steer him away from that spot. It didn't often
work and I now realize that he was right in his contention that
a plant that had begun to grow badly could never be made into
a decent citizen and the only thing to do was to scrap it.*
MARGERY FISH, 'WE MADE A GARDEN'.

Mrs Fish was reputedly devoted to her husband. No doubt
she had her reasons.

A somewhat easier working relationship is implicit in the
splendid books written by Anne Scott-James and illustrated
by her husband, Osbert Lancaster, though the author did
comment in 'The Pleasure Garden' (a brief history of gardening in England) that the illustrator's predilection for drawing
yuccas made him a little unreliable in the chapters on Roman
Britain. Miss Scott-James' prose is at all times admirable;
concise, scholarly, down-to-earth and drily entertaining.

Her latest book, an anthology of garden writing called 'The
Language of the Garden', contains what is possibly my
favourite piece of all:

Painting the Roses White

*O*n this situation the only adequate response is to thank God for chemical pesticides, and use them liberally. Unfortunately the strongest and most effective ones keep being withdrawn from the market on the grounds that they have been found to damage the environment. So when you hit on a really lethal source it's a good plan to buy it in large supply, which will enable you to go on using it after it has been outlawed. I did this for several seasons with a splendid product, now alas unobtainable, which wiped out everything from snails to flea beetles. It had no adverse effect on the bird population as far as I could see, though the neighbourhood cats did start to look a bit seedy. That, of course, was an advantage from my point of view, for cats are filthy, insanitary beasts, and a fearful nuisance to the gardener. One of the anomalies of English law is that whereas it would, as I understand it, be an offence to clamber over your neighbour's fence and defecate among his vegetables, you can send a feline accomplice on precisely the same errand with total impunity. It has always amazed me that manufacturers of slug bait, and other such garden aids, should proudly announce on the label that their product is 'harmless to pets'. A pesticide that could guarantee to cause pets irreparable damage would, I'd have thought, sell like hot cakes.

JOHN CAREY, 'THE PLEASURES OF VEGETABLE GARDENING' IN ANNE SCOTT-JAMES' ANTHOLOGY 'THE LANGUAGE OF THE GARDEN'.

These forthright views about pesticides are evidently shared by two American gardeners, Henry Beard and Roy McKie:

*I*nsecticides. A new respect for the environment and stricter regulations have taken most of the effective, but

destructive, poisons off the shelf and replaced them with more
benign, but less potent, compounds. Typical of the new
insecticides are Annoyene, which gives some caterpillars a mild
itching sensation; Migrene, which gives slugs a headache; and
Dorene, Norene, and Charlene, a family of aromatic hydro-
carbons based on inexpensive perfumes that have a vague
repellent effect on grubs, chiggers, and mites.

HENRY BEARD AND ROY MCKIE, 'GAR.DEN.ING. A GARDENER'S
DICTIONARY'.

These same gentlemen were the source of my early instruction
in the art of topiary:

*T*opiary. The art of pruning and shearing plants so that
they resemble animals. It is not as difficult as you might
think. Avoid deer, swans, giraffes, and bears. Concentrate your
efforts on depicting sponges, porcupines, frightened turtles, and
sleeping hedgehogs.

They are also masters of the one-liner:

*L*ily of the Field. Attractive, unemployed, non-textile
producing flower.
   Hose. Crude, but effective and totally safe type of scythe
towed through gardens to flatten flower beds and level vegetable
plantings.

They don't have this field on their own, though. Hardy Amies
turns a nice phrase:

I am calmly extravagant about tulips.
HARDY AMIES IN 'THE ENGLISHMAN'S GARDEN'.

Harold Nicholson also produced some very quotable quotes:

Vita only likes flowers which are brown and difficult to grow.

HAROLD NICHOLSON, QUOTED BY ANNE SCOTT-JAMES IN 'SISSINGHURST'.

All these titbits are, of course, only a hint, the merest soupçon of the huge enjoyment to be had from that old standby, a good book in front of the winter fire. But at some point, even in the bitterest weather, every gardener will feel the urge for the real thing, and will forsake the warmth and the printed word for a spell of hands-on:

Weeds have begun to show themselves in the beds and are quite easy to root out—ground is soft from the rains. I get at this every chance I can. When I decide to go at them in earnest, I try to make myself as comfortable as possible. That way, I'll stick to it longer. I put on a couple of layers of clothes, which I can shed if the sun warms me and the wind stops. I also have an old pair of wool gloves with holes in the fingers, which are perfect for weeding. And since my nose always seems to be running when I am out of doors this time of year, a good pocketful of tissues. I paint a lovely picture, don't I? You wouldn't know it to look at me, but I am happy as a clam.

LEE BAILEY, 'COUNTRY FLOWERS'.

While this is a mollusc with which I am not overly familiar, I nonetheless feel quite safe in asserting that so am I, Mr Bailey, so am I.

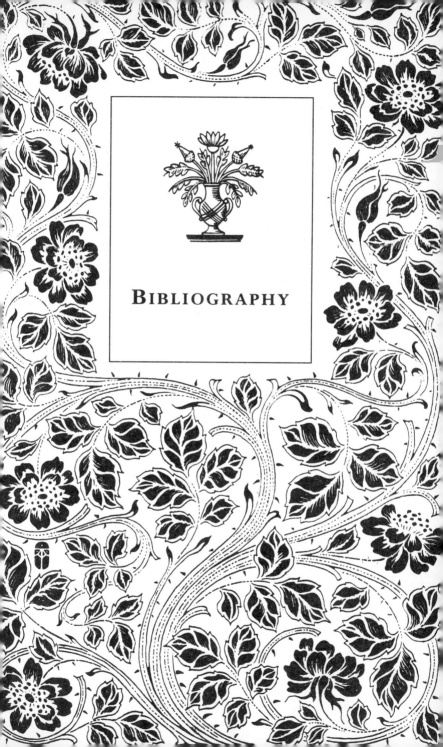

BIBLIOGRAPHY

Bibliography

Bailey, L. *Country Flowers* (Clarkson N. Potter, 1985).

Beard, H. and McKie, R. *gar.den.ing. A Gardener's Dictionary* (First published Workman Publishing Company, 1982; Sun Books edition, 1982).

Buchan, U. *An Anthology of Garden Writing* (Croom Helm, 1986).

Fish, M. *We Made a Garden* (First published W. H. and L. Collingridge Ltd, 1956; Faber and Faber edition, 1983).

Gault, S. M. and Singe, P. M. *The Dictionary of Roses in Colour* (Mermaid Books, 1971).

Griffiths, T. *My World of Old Roses*, Vol. 2 (Nelson, 1986).

Hitchmough, J. *Gardener's Choice* (Kangaroo Press, 1987).

Jekyl, G. *Wood and Garden* (Macmillan, Papermac edition, 1983).
——, *Colour Schemes for the Flower Garden* (Country Life, 4th edition, 1919).

Lees-Milne, A. and Verey, R. *The Englishwoman's Garden* (Chatto and Windus, 1980).
——, *The Englishman's Garden* (Penguin, 1982).

Lloyd, C. *The Adventurous Gardener* (First published Allen Lane, 1983; Penguin edition, 1985).
——, *The Well-Chosen Garden* (First published Elm Tree Books/Hamish Hamilton, 1984; Mermaid Books edition, 1985).

Painting the Roses White

——, *The Well-Tempered Garden* (First published William Collins, 1970, revised edition, Viking, 1985).

Masson, G. *Italian Gardens* (First published Thames and Hudson, 1961; revised edition, Antique Collectors' Club, 1987).

McMaugh, J. *What Garden Pest or Disease Is That?* (Lansdowne Press, 1985).

Nichols, B. *Down the Garden Path* (Jonathan Cape, 1936).

Page, R. *The Education of a Gardener* (First published Collins, 1962; Penguin edition, 1985).

Perry, F. and Seale, A. *Gardening in Colour* (Hamlyn for *The Australian Women's Weekly*, 1967).

Scott-James, A. *Sissinghurst: The Making of a Garden* (Michael Joseph, 1975),
——, *The Language of the Garden* (First published Viking, 1984; Penguin edition, 1987).
——, *The Pleasure Garden* (First published John Murray, 1977; Penguin edition, 1979).

Tolley, E. and Mead, C. *Herbs* (Sidgwick and Jackson, 1985).

Verey, R. *Classic Garden Design* (The Viking Press, 1984).

Yates Garden Guide (Angus & Robertson, 1992).